Exile
in Literature

Exile
in Literature

Edited by
María-Inés Lagos-Pope

Lewisburg
Bucknell University Press
London and Toronto: Associated University Presses

© 1988 by Associated University Presses, Inc.

Associated University Presses
440 Forsgate Drive
Cranbury, NJ 08512

Associated University Presses
25 Sicilian Avenue
London WC1A 2QH, England

Associated University Presses
P.O. Box 488, Port Credit
Mississauga, Ontario
Canada L5G 4M2

Library of Congress Cataloging-in-Publication Data

Exile in literature.

Includes bibliographies.
Contents: Introduction / María-Inés Lagos-Pope—
Exile, self, and society / Robert Edwards—Exile as
salvation in Hrotswitha's Paphnutius / Sandro
Sticca—[etc.]
1. Exiles in literature. I. Lagos-Pope, María-Inés,
date— .
PN56.5.E96E96 1988   809'.93355   87-47726
ISBN 0-8387-5126-1 (alk. paper)

The paper used in this publication meets the requirements
of the American National Standard for Permanence of Paper
for Printed Library Materials Z39.48-1984.

Printed in the United States of America

Contents

Introduction

MARIA-INES LAGOS-POPE

Since antiquity the term exile has been associated with the idea of loss or separation. Discussions treating this concept have focused on both the idea of being separated from a place and from the self, as Robert Edwards shows in "Exile, Self, and Society," the essay that opens this volume.

In its various forms, exile has been a recurrent human experience. In his lengthy study on exile, Paul Tabori has traced the history of exiles from the first documented case, that of the Egyptian Sinuhe, who lived around 2000 B.C., to the various exile groups of the twentieth century. Since exile acquires different connotations depending on the historical period and other specific circumstances, Tabori does not propose just one definition of exile but rather examines individual cases and periods.

Perhaps more than any other period in history, the twentieth century has witnessed an enormous flow of displaced people. Examples range from the Europeans who fled from the Nazis, to the more recent Asians and Latin Americans who migrated to escape war, dictatorial regimes, and/or famine. Exile has become a common occurrence. The public is only too familiar with the plight of the Soviet dissidents, the Cubans from Mariel, the various African groups who have had to flee their homelands or who have been sent to internal exile, the Vietnamese-American children who are being resettled in the United States, and so on.

It is significant and not coincidental that among the most recent Nobel prize winners for literature one finds several exiles. Elias Canetti, the 1981 winner, is a Bulgarian who writes in German and lives in London. Czeslaw Milosz, who was awarded the prize in 1980 and who specifically referred to exile in his Nobel lecture, is a former Polish diplomat who now teaches in California, and the 1978 winner, the Polish-born American Isaac Bashevis Singer, writes in Yiddish. Previous Nobel Prize recipients who have lived in exile part or most of their lives, include Vladimir Nabokov, Samuel Beckett, Pablo Neruda, Juan Ramón Jiménez, and Miguel Angel Asturias.

The Argentinian author Julio Cortázar, who lived most of his life in

France first as a voluntary exile and later as a true exile banned from his country, has observed that for many Latin American writers exile has become not only a fact of life and a literary theme, but a leitmotiv of Latin American reality and literature. For the creative artist exile is an especially traumatic experience, not just because of the physical displacement from the native land but because his or her professional tools are inextricably related to the cultural and linguistic realities of his/her country of origin. As a result of this situation, there have been numerous gatherings and symposia devoted to discussing and addressing the specific needs of the diaspora among Latin American authors and intellectuals, in order to maintain some kind of cohesion and provide opportunities for publicizing new works written in exile. A group of Chilean exiles, for instance, has published since 1977 a literary review called *Literatura Chilena en el Exilio.*

Given these realities, and the fact that throughout history exiles have expressed their experiences through writing, it seems pertinent to delve into the ways in which exile has been represented in literature and study how it has been articulated and transformed in a literary work. This book has its origins in a lecture series sponsored by the Department of Romance Languages and Literatures at SUNY-Binghamton under the direction of Professor Sandro Sticca and myself in the 1980–81 academic year. The present collection includes some of the papers originally read at the series, and others that were explicitly sollicited for the volume.

In the opening essay, "Exile, Self, and Society," Robert Edwards provides an overview of the concept of exile from its historical definition to the applications of metaphor and theme. After examining works by Ovid and Dante, *El Poema de Mío Cid,* and texts from medieval vernacular literatures, the author offers three modes of the poetic transformation of exile. The first concerns "the function of memory," which has the power to transform the original experience by viewing it from a different perspective; the second refers to the creation of an alternate society, much like the one found in *El Poema de Mío Cid* in which Ruy Díz attempts to form a new kingdom beyond Christian territory; and the third concerns the imaginary projection toward the future, as is evidenced by Dante, who "recurs to imagination . . . as an activity of mind where the historical reality of exile reveals its full meaning to a self still enmeshed in contingency."

The purpose of this collection is to explore different modes and applications of the concept of exile as expressed in western literary works of various origins, namely German, Irish, Italian, Latin, Latin American, Spanish, and of different periods, emphasizing the rhetoric of exile. The articles focus on works from the classical period to the present and examine exile from a wide range of perspectives: from exile understood in a strict sense, with its implications of forced banishment from one's own country, as in the case of Dante or Miguel de Unamuno, to a metaphorical interpretation of the term, such as that of Hrotswitha of Gandersheim. Between these two poles different utilizations of the concept can be observed, which range from internal exile to a national trait, as is exemplified in the essays that focus on German literature and modern Irish poetry, respectively. While this volume was in its developmental stages several studies treating the subject of exile appeared. The most significant are those of Edward Said—his chapter "Secular Criticism" in *The World, the Text, and the Critic* (1983), and his essay "The Mind of Winter: Reflections on Life in Exile" (*Harper's*, September 1984)—and Michael Seidel's *Exile and the Narrative Imagination* (1986).

In Christianity the concept of exile was often used to refer to man's life on earth. As exiles from heaven, their true home or destination, Christians had to act according to God's will and live free from worldly temptations in order to earn their place in paradise. One example of this application of the term is Sandro Sticca's analysis of Hrotswitha of Gandersheim's play, *Paphnutius*. Sticca suggests that the central theme and metaphor in the play is penitential exile, understood as solitary confinement in order to achieve "spiritual progress and contemplative union with God." Sticca demonstrates that exile assumes both religious and aesthetic significance in Hroswitha's work.

A metaphorical use of the concept of exile is represented by twentieth-century Irish authors. According to George O'Brien's interpretation, exile, considered as "a movement of the mind, a cultural reaction, a metonym for the restlessness, disaffection, isolation and self-respect," defines and characterizes the aesthetic and spiritual position of the modern Irish writer. Dante's *Divine Comedy* offers a view of exile on the threshold between the metaphorical use of the term and true exile as a result of political banishment. As Giuseppe Mazzotta has shown in his essay, exile is not just a theme in *The Divine Comedy* but a "radical metaphor" for the poem. The critic suggests that Boccaccio's desire to bring home to Florence the "spirit" of the poet by returning Dante's ashes that lie in Ravenna to his native city reveals a misunderstanding of Dante's own insight that exile be his irreducible personal experience. In his examination of two related scenes in *Inferno* 15 and *Paradiso* 15–28, Mazzotta indicates that for Dante exile becomes a necessary perspective. Through his reading of the song of exile, "Three Women Have Come Round My Heart," he shows that Dante understands exile not only as a contingent historical reality but as the condition of man on this earth. Furthermore, in the representation of the three theological virtues, Faith, Hope and Charity, in *Paradiso* 24, 25, and 26, respectively, the critic finds systematic references, explicit and oblique, to exile.

In the twentieth century totalitarian regimes have produced a different type of exile often called internal exile. The distinction between expatriation and internal exile has been recognized, and both have been practiced since ancient times. And, as Robert Edwards points out, for Cicero "exile can occur without one's being driven from a home." In modern times, the idea of internal exile was developed in Germany to refer to those citizens who, even though they stayed in their country during the Nazi period, rejected and opposed National Socialism in a variety of ways. This phenomenon has given rise to controversial debates and has not been readily accepted or recognized as a form of true exile, as there is no physical displacement, no uprootedness, and no separation from one's own culture, language, and history. In her paper, Rosmarie Morewedge demonstrates that spiritual exile was an alternative to physical exile and constituted ideological resistance when other options were not feasible. In her opinion *innere Emigration* did constitute a channel for expressing disagreement with a repressive totalitarian regime without the risk of death and thus should be considered a legitimate form of exile, as can be seen in Heinrich Boell's novel *Billiards at Half Past Nine.* This discussion is especially pertinent since the idea it promulgates has been applied to situations experienced in other countries, such as Spain and Argentina, to signify the type of exile that some individuals suffered under Franco and others under Argentina's military government from 1976 to 1983.

A case of a true exile in the Hispanic world is that of Miguel de Unamuno, who was deported from Spain in 1924 by the government of Primo de Rivera. While exiled in Paris he wrote a novel entitled *Cómo se hace una novela,* which was first published in Jean Cassou's French translation. In 1927, Unamuno rewrote the novel by translating the French version into Spanish and making a number of new additions, which he kept in parentheses. Randolph Pope's essay proposes a new reading of this text, regarding it as "a description of the experience of exile." This approach enables the author to elucidate the contradictions that critics have found in the novel and provides convincing arguments explaining why Unamuno chose to write an unfinished novel. Pope suggests that what Unamuno wanted to show was the experience of exile. "A finished novel would have given the illusion of accomplishment, precisely what he wished to short-circuit, because it would have made his exile look creative." In the final entry, "Testimonies from Exile," I examine three narratives that were written in exile. Their narrators are Latin American exiles who give accounts of the circumstances that pushed them into banishment. All three describe totalitarian systems of government that exclude intellectuals or writers because they invite subversion. For this reason exile is their only choice.

In order to emphasize the existence of a tradition and the historical utilization of the concept of exile, the essays have been arranged in chronological order, although they could have been divided in a different way. They could, for example, have been grouped into two main categories. The first would include those essays that use the term metaphorically, and here we could distinguish between the Christian concept that sees exile as the condition of the soul longing for rest in God and the representation of spiritual alienation. The second group would comprise those studies which deal with the representation of exile as a consequence of concrete banishment. Yet, such a clear-cut division would not reflect the complex realities and experiences that the term exile encompasses and would obscure the rhetoric of exile, which assumes many modes and forms and is at the center of these essays. Exile speaks, but through the texts.

I would like to express special thanks to Professor Sandro Sticca for his invaluable assistance and encouragement in the preparation of this volume.

Exile
in Literature

Exile, Self, and Society

ROBERT EDWARDS

Since the notion of exile lends itself to so many forms of expression in medieval literature, it might be useful to begin my discussion by considering a poetic model of exile. The model I have in mind is one of the maxims excerpted from the now lost mimes of the Roman writer Publilius Syrus (fl. 45 B.C.) and circulated in the schoolbooks of antiquity and the Middle Ages as an independent text. Publilius writes of exile, "Exilium patitur patriae qui se denegat."[1] J. Wight Duff, taking *patriae* as a dative with the verb *denegare,* translates: "He suffers exile who denies himself to his country."[2] An alternate rendering, which preserves the order of the phrasing, brings the public and private dimensions of exile into heightened relief: "He suffers exile from his homeland who denies himself." Publilius's maxim is also an example of what it seeks to define. It is itself twice exiled, removed from the surrounding context of the original dramatic work and even from its historical period. As a proverb, it is a drifting verbal construction sufficient in its own meaning yet adaptable to various contexts. Nonetheless it captures what seem to be the essential terms and relations of exile.

Publilius's fugitive line, however we choose to construe it, concentrates the ideas and terms of exile developed elsewhere by classical and medieval writers as a metaphor, theme, and component of narrative structure. Under various guises, exile means separation, banishment, withdrawal, expatriation, and displacement; its emotional expression is loss, usually manifested as sorrow, though sometimes as nostalgia. Moreover, the link between event and affect seems inherent. We might speak superficially of "undergoing exile," but language inevitably carries us toward registering the feelings of suffering and enduring displacement from one's "home." Only by a willful suppression of metaphor can we speak of "experiencing exile." Otherwise language continues to seek forceful expression, as in one's being driven, thrown, or cast into exile.

The derivation of the Latin term *exsilium* shows clearly that disjunction is essential to the notion of exile, but scholars are less certain whether the stress falls on an act of separation *(salire, saltare)* or the place from which one is divided *(ex solo,* "from native ground"). Ernout and Meillet incline toward the latter as the preference of Latin writers, and Cicero *(Paradoxa Stoicorum* 4.2.31) gives indirect support of that usage, explaining that miscreants and the impious are exiles, even if they do not change their dwellings ("etiamsi solum non mutarint").[3] Isidore of Seville *(Etymologiae* 5.27.28) derives the term from "extra solum." In Publilius's maxim, the phrasing leaves no doubt about the division from one's homeland *(exilium patriae),* nor does the collateral use of *exsilium* in classical Latin to mean "a place of exile."[4] In a broader view, however, this break is not simply with space or location but with the cultural and social continuities of place and with a collective history. Duff's translation of Publilius makes central a role for the state by equating exile with denying oneself to one's country as a source of paternity and lineage. The idea of self based on personal identity thus plays against a self defined by consensus and verified in the roles and repetitions of social life.

Besides the civic emphases of a republican and imperial state, there is in most classical and medieval thinking about exile a sense of alienation from the self. Publilius speaks directly of denying or rejecting oneself, and in the famous *Ode* celebrating the leisure of his farm and his own poetic gifts, Horace asks, "Patriae quis exsul / se quoque fugit" ("What exile from his country has ever fled himself?" [2.16.19–20]). Ovid likewise extends the separation from place into self-alienation, fusing the two in his description of the frenzied Alcmeon as "exsul mentis domusque" ("an exile from mind and home" [*Metamorphoses* 9.409]). His link between madness and exile anticipates later treatments of Biblical and classical figures by medieval writers who connect sin and insanity with banishment and flight.[5] But the more revealing usage lies in the domain of Christian rather than classical values. The denial of self that Latin writers equate with civic exile paradoxically becomes in Christ's admonition to his disciples a means of salvation— that is, of regaining oneself: "Si quis vult post me sequi deneget se ipsum" ("If anyone wishes to follow me, let him deny himself" [Mark 8:34]).[6] St. Paul carries the notion from questions of identity to the realm of the spirit, arguing in 2 Corinthians 5:6 that man's corporeal existence is a separation from the Lord ("peregrinamur a Domino") reparable by his walking in faith rather than by sight. In its most profound implications, the literature of exile depends precisely on devising ways to walk in faith despite historical contingencies.

The linguistic dimensions of *exsilium* reveal a set of terms whose connections I want to examine in a certain breadth. These connections reflect the possibilities or permutations given within what are at times specific designations of the terms. The eidetic structure of exile is an uprooting from native soil and translation from the center to the periphery, from organized space invested with meaning to a boundary where the conditions of experience are problematic. For historians and critics the affective component of this change proves the central concern. The fact of exile tests notions of self and social order, and as it does so each of the terms transforms. Exile does not simply magnify personal separation to a collective displacement; rather, it intensifies the dialectical relation of the individual within the social. We shall look first to some of the historical permutations where exile defines a specific relation of self and society. These historical cases offer a grounding for the poetic treatment. Yet by its very nature, exile is a psychological experience, a response of mind and spirit to customs, codes, and political actions; and so its qualities have to be measured by the figures projected on the historical ground. Thus our main interests will lie in the expansions toward metaphor and sources of poetic transformation.

In his *Anatomy of Exile,* Paul Tabori finds the earliest historical example of exile in the flight of the Egyptian Sinuhe about 2000 B.C. Hearing that he is to be seized by authorities, Sinuhe flees the kingdom and spends his life among aliens, returning only as an old man who seeks Pharaoh's mercy.[7] As a judicial and political measure, enforced banishment affords a means to assure peace and stability without direct violence or the imposition of penalties; in short, it allows the state to temper its decisions without compromising underlying principles or authority. Aristotle (*Constitution of Athens* 22) credits Cleisthenes with the invention of ostracism whereby a vote of citizens could force ten years' exile without criminal charges or the loss of property. Historians connect the measure with the transition from tribal structures to the city state and its democratic institutions. Apart from this political measure, banishment or flight becomes the fate of tragedians like Aeschylus and Euripides, who use voluntary retirement to escape defeat and satire, and of Aristotle himself, who avoids charges of impiety and saves Athens from committing a second offense against philosophy (the first was Socrates' death) by leaving the city of his own will. As in the Middle Ages, banishment can also be a mechanism of economic growth, drawing the energies of ambitious men toward the margins of the state and validating pillage as an instrument of expansion.

Under Roman law, exile allows individuals and the state flexibility in evading capital punishment after legal processes have established guilt. During the Republic, a citizen can escape the death penalty by flight. Thereafter an *interdictio aqua et igni* follows, and the guilty party remains liable to be put to death should he return. From the age of Tiberius onwards, this interdiction included the loss of citizenship and property.[8] Deportation could replace interdiction with the effect "not only that the convicted person became a *peregrinus,* but that he was confined to an island or oasis, and lost the whole of his property except such amount as might be left to him as an act of grace."[9] A milder form of exile was *relegatio,* imposed temporarily or for life, which forced residence outside a specified location or in a fixed place but without loss of citizenship and property.

Exile was a punishment reserved for the upper classes; for the lower, the corresponding penalty was a life sentence of forced labor. The *Lex Romana Burgundionum* of the fifth century A.D. preserves the difference among classes long after juridical culture had declined in the provinces: "Honestiores persone damnantur exilio, uiliores uero metallis deputantur" ("The more respectable persons are condemned to exile, but the common people are sent to the mines").[10] In the "libri terribiles" of Justinian's *Digest* (48.22.5), so called because they deal with criminal law, exile can take three forms: "aut certorum locorum interdictio; aut lata fuga, ut omnium locorum interdicatur praeter certum locum, aut insulae uinculum, id est relegatio in insulam" ("either an interdiction of a certain place; or broad flight, as when one is forbidden every place rather than a certain locality; or confinement to an island, that is, relegation to an island").

History and law combine enforced banishment and voluntary withdrawals in a single term. In certain respects, this combination exemplifies the overlay of compulsion and will in exile. Sinuhe's flight, like the retirements of the poets and philosophers, is an individual decision, but it incorporates a choice already limited by circumstances. Exile can also involve withdrawal as a means to gain or learn something, and such retreat is often the prelude to change. Language attempts to express these subtleties and refinements with supplementary terms. Some usage associates voluntary exile with *demigratio, fuga,* and *peregrinatio;* forced exile becomes, in addition to the legal designations, *expulsio* or *eiectio.* Grappling with the legal distinction, commentators on Vergil debate whether the opening lines of his epic, especially the phrase "fato profugus" ("banished by fate"), describe voluntary or involuntary flight. Donatus, for example, remarks that Aeneas, having left his native homeland, was carried into foreign lands "as if an exile" (*In Aeneidos Commentaria* 1.2). Isidore (*De differentiis verborum* 1.452) proposes a compromise view that in fact restores the original distinction without accounting for the underlying differences: "profugus voluntate, exul necessitate" ("a wanderer by choice, an exile by necessity"). Medieval Latin expands *exilium* beyond the distinction of forced and voluntary displacement so that it also means devastation, destruction, waste, and ruin. *Exsul* similarly comes to mean a wanderer, pilgrim, or outlaw.[12] The Romance languages follow in the direction of these added denotations, with Old French *essil,* Provençal *essilh,* and Catalan *exill* meaning exile, devastation, and torment.[13]

The expansion of direct meaning has its counterpart in the proliferations of metaphor where positive description gives way to uses that reflect conceptual and imaginative possibilities. While it can be traced historically, the metaphor of exile has its great value in showing us not only what but how writers see. In many cases, the dual perspective has to do with a cultural shift. Christian writers, for example, amplify the juridical and political dimensions of exile in order to define mankind's place in the world and to set history on an ontological ground. Tertullian, Augustine, and Gregory use the term to refer to Adam's expulsion from Paradise, and Sulpicius Severus (*Chronicon* 1.22) echoes the legal vocabulary of banishment in saying, "Adam et Eva in nostram velut exules terram eiecti sunt" ("Adam and Eve were driven into our world like exiles"). Jerome's Vulgate designates Cain "vagus et profugus," an exile from the face of God who subsequently founds the first city and names it after his son (Genesis 4:12–17). In religious lyric, the "Salve Regina" sees all men as "exules filii Evae." Ecclesiastical writers apply *exilium* to the wanderings of the Jews after Christ's death, thereby bringing the Babylonian Captivity and the disaspora into accord and shaping a cultural history around displacement and loss. Commenting on the Book of Isaiah, Jerome fashions Israel "totius orbis exul atque peregrinus"—terms which urge not only movement but perpetual residence in foreign lands. The Wandering Jew of the Middle Ages concentrates this collective history in a single figure. In a different vein, Honorius of Autun and Hugh of St. Victor connect the exile of man's being on earth to the act of reading.[14]

Augustine lends a figurative sense to the classical insistence on separation from a homeland (*solum*) by locating spiritual exile in a "Land of Unlikeness" (*Confessions* 7.10), which is situated between nothing and the perfected being of God: "Your light shone upon me in its brilliance, and I thrilled with love and dread alike. I realized that I was far away from you. It was as though I were in a land where all is different from your own and I heard your voice calling from on high, saying, 'I am the food of full-grown men. Grow and you shall feed on me. But you shall not change me into your own substance, as you do with the food of your body. Instead you shall be changed into me.' "[15] St. Bernard subsequently modifies Augustine's notion and its Platonic associations to evoke a region of exile where man's sins result in the deformity of his made likeness to God and in a curvature from the divine back toward the earthly.

Etienne Gilson explains this conjunction of alienation and the metaphor of exile in Bernard: "Wandering, hopelessly revolving, in the 'circuit of the impious' those who tread this weary round suffer not only the loss of God but also the loss of themselves. They dare no longer look their own souls in the face; could they do it they would no longer recognize themselves. For when the soul has lost its likeness to God it is no longer like itself: *inde anima dissimilis/ Deo dissimilis/ est et sibi;* a likeness which is no longer like its original is like itself no more."[16] It is to this metaphor of exile that Beatrice returns in explaining divine justice to Dante in the Heaven of Mercury (*Paradiso,* 5–7). Man's timebound spiritual illness, she reasons, has left his nature removed from its maker ("la natura che dal suo fattore / s'era allungata" [7.31–32], and it alone has effected his banishment from Paradise ("ma per se stessa fu ella sbandita / di Paradiso" [7.37–38]).

The expansions of primary meaning and metaphor point toward still broader thematic connections. Beyond framing experience in the language of separation and loss, exile allows writers to construct sustained fictive worlds whose alterity or betweenness requires aesthetic rationales and poetic justice. At the same time, however, exile brings to bear certain formal problems in the writing of narrative, particularly in writing a unified work. Banishment and withdrawal lead to adventure, discovery, and eventual resolution; but this tripartite structure centers on what Aristotle would call character rather than plot. It drifts toward episodic structure or adapts the strategies of ideological and chronological narrative developed in classical biography.[17] For the narrative of exile, the formal problem lies in devising continuities that join personality and action, such as in elegy, national epic, and allegory. At a stylistic level, the problem is analogous to the original fall from grace: the sum of all songs of exile will not restore one to the homeland, and when writers create an imaginary home, the effect may be a further alienation. A language constructed in the past tense portrays diminished expectations, for the present is less golden than what has happened before. When it offers better things, language moves from predicaments to predicables. At the furthest reach, the result is that language becomes abstract and philosophical.

The theme of exile thus developed in classical and medieval narrative takes various forms of expression. As we have seen, Augustine and Bernard propose that to the degree one is separated from God, one is exiled from oneself. In an organic view, the separation of mind and sense from the body and their replacement by passions constitute exile. The medieval portrayals of Nebuchadnezzar and Chrétien de Troyes's description of Yvain's "folie" treat a collapse into man's lower faculties and a compulsive relegation to nature.[18] Alternately, this kind of exile supports mystical experience and carries into a spiritual realm Plato's insistence that the philosopher must remove mind from the organism. Tabori and others, following Erik Erikson's developmental psychology, argue that exile attacks identity by threatening continuity and one's ability to project a self located in time and space confidently toward the future. Yet Augustine (*De trinitate* 11) holds out greater prospects by defining personality as a fusion of memory, will, and intellect, much as Plato (*Philebus* 34a–39d) had earlier hypothesized a conservation of perceptions. The classical and medieval thinkers escape psychological determinism by their emphasis on will and expectation.

Separations from family and country involve an interesting thematic ambivalence in medieval literature. The prime consequence of losing social institutions is to remove external definitions of self, but its secondary effect can be the creation or discovery of a new personality. The Old French *Vie de Saint Alexis* conceives its protagonist's exile from family and marriage as a necessary withdrawal resulting at length in affirmations that Alexis is a man of God. The first part of the eleventh-century poem covers Alexis's leaving on his wedding night and living for seventeen years as a beggar until an image proclaims his sanctity. The second part recounts Alexis's escape from popular recognition and an unforeseen return to Rome, where he lives another seventeen years unrecognized under the stairs of his family's home. The structural doubling suggests the equivalence of flight and internal alienation, much as Cicero had earlier stipulated that exile can occur without one's being driven from a home. It also protracts a middle period bounded on one side by a willful segregation from family and on the other by a reintegration signalled by God and honored by the Emperor and Pope, who read Alexis's history and bury him.

The parabolic shape of exile in Alexis's history exaggerates what Victor Turner has identified as the "liminal phase" in ritual structures. The period after separation and before one rejoins society accentuates an awareness of being "betwixt and between"; it is a "realm of pure possibility whence novel configurations of ideas and relations may arise."[19] In narrative, the period coincides with the symbolic geography of a threshold between organized space and the wasteland outside. The dialectics of inside and outside, center and periphery release one from previous definitions. Seen in these terms, exile takes over the function of a construct where time and space converge to shape a new personality. The essence of this shaping, as Turner insists, is hypothesis and speculation. It is not enough merely to reject what one has been because denial alone preserves the original norms; one has to posit something tentative in their place even when, as is the case in archaic societies, the process of experiment is cyclical and succeeds in returning one to a place within traditional organization.[20] Apart from its application to personal histories, the betweenness of exile fosters myths of culture that integrate new elements within the old when compelled by historical necessity.

The theme of exile touches not only personal and cultural history but also the process of artistic creation. Poetic banishment represents an exile from grace and from the craft or occupation that has made it possible for the writer to devise works. It is separation from a visionary company joined by a common language. The classical paradigm for such exile is the experience that Ovid presents as he records his banishment from Rome in the *Tristia* and *Epistulae ex Ponto*. At various stages, his elegies mention the immediate and concrete forms of exile—afflictions of the organism through physical illness and mental distress; separations from wife, family, friends, and place; the loss of reputation, civic standing, and prospects for the future. But a recurrent concern of these works—what lends resonance to their tedious supplication of friends and Emperor—is the relation of poetic genius to exile. Ovid recognizes the precarious dual nature of his books. While they give him delight and a measure of solace in his relegation to the Black Sea, they are also the source of his injury (*Tristia* 4.1). His exile is caused by the products of his genius, and in some respects the books have acted as parricides, not unlike Oedipus and Telegonus (*Tristia* 1.1). Still, their complicity in his banishment from society proves less important than their capacity to witness his survival.

The *Tristia* opens with the poet sending the book to Rome in order to salute those who remember him and to say that the poet still lives. Book Three similarly describes itself as "the book of a trembling exile" returned to the city (3.1). Ovid personifies his work, substituting the text for its author, so as to suggest that art may offer the only remedy to exile.[21] Amid his repeated pleas for mercy and intercession with the Emperor, he counsels one friend to remember him not by a likeness stamped in a ring but by reading his verse (1.7). Other friends presumably abandon him, but their loss is balanced by Ovid's role in a community of poets and the Muses (1.9). Thus his invocations to the Muse are both prayers for grace and attempts to integrate the poet back into a realm from which his work has become estranged. A letter to Perilla develops this line of thought by urging devotion to the Muse as a means to insure immortality and constancy (3.7). The Muse allows Ovid to live surrounded by calamity, offering companionship and a release from the oppression of exile through imagination. But if art helps to modify his suffering, it is nonetheless a frail rescue; for the poet's language—the coinage of urbanity—grows barbarous and he must practice its preservation consciously (5.7, 5.12, *Epistula* 1.5), aware all the time that his removal from a sophisticated society to a primitive one lures him into not polishing the lines and to composing in a foreign tongue.

The link between poetic creation and banishment that emerges from Ovid's late works provides a conceptual approach to what is probably the most concentrated treatment of exile in the medieval vernacular literatures. Without being a direct source, Ovid helps us to gauge the thematic and narrative developments of exile within Old English poetry. Translated to a heroic rather than urbane society, his emphasis on the ambivalent nature of poetry, the isolation from community, and the vulnerability of human achievements acquires a new specificity rooted in the literature of a culture that insistently views itself in retrospect. With Ovid's admission that genius caused his banishment to the edges of civilization we might compare the narrowed and concrete assertion that a poet is necessarily a wanderer. Among his extensive mnemonic lists of heroes, rulers, and tribes, the fictional *scop* Widsith (the "far journeyer") recounts his own position as one "who of men had fared through most races and peoples over the earth":

"Thus I travelled through many foreign lands, through this wide world; good and evil I suffered there, cut off from kinsmen, far from those of my blood; I served far and wide." Like Ovid, he is separated from family, companions and lineage; and his suffering arises from the emotional disjunction. Again like Ovid, he joins the disparate experiences of his exile by a theme of return in which gifts and praise can restore his position, his land, and "my father's dwelling-place." Yet the spacial matrix of exile allows Widsith to encompass an entire racial history and to convert the exaggerations of myth and chronology into a single consciousness located in the poet. "The minstrels of men go wandering," he realizes, "as fate directs, through many lands; they utter their need, speak the word of thanks."[22]

A second poem about a displaced minstrel-poet from the Exeter Book offers variations on these themes within a lyrical-narrative structure. *Deor,* like *Widsith,* maintains a dual focus on heroic action and exile. In his allusions to Germanic legend, the speaker narrows the distance between a collective history and his present situation. Weland's story, which begins the list of allusions, foreshadows the poet's destiny in substituting for human companions the companionship of sorrow and longing *(hæfde him to gesiþþe sorge ond longaþ).* His exile prefigures the expulsion suffered by the poet at the end of the work when another bard assumes his claims to land and protection. Moreover, in the iteration of the terms *wræces* and *wintercealde wræce,* the poem reveals the conversion of banishment to its psychological equivalents in a single word—*wræc*—that means both "exile" and "misery." This conversion occurs within a broader pattern of change governed by a wise Lord *(witig Dryhten)* who apportions fate and fortune. The poet's refrain—þæs ofereode, þisses swa mæg ("That passed away, so will this")— frames heroic and poetic exile within mutability that promises either to outlast suffering or to render it meaningless in a new dimension.

The classical and medieval treatments of exile that I have mentioned suggest that beneath the morphology of theme, exile forces certain modes of literary transformation. Whatever the situation it describes, the medieval literature of exile remains centered on change. To some extent change is implicit in any poetic vision, for the mutual translations of art and experience reconceive both the world and the possibilities of expressing it. Within a narrower dialectic, though, change appears as a consequence of exile and seeks to revise the terms that give rise to separation. That is, literature concerned with banishment and flight contains within itself certain remedies of estrangement: it is never enough merely to record loss. Thus we must consider not only the relations of exile, self, and society, but additionally, the modes of poetic transformation brought to each of them; and in this appraisal we would do well to keep in mind that poetry at once projects a fictive world and helps to describe an empirical one. Its historical character is necessarily dual—mimetic and constitutive. This dichotomy persists through what I take to be three important modes of transformation connected to exile in medieval texts.

The first of these modes involves the function of memory within exile. Scholars who view the Homeric poems as an effort to preserve a pre-Doric culture driven to Asia Minor posit a decisive role for memory in a literature based on disjunction. Such a literature conserves the records of custom and deeds, but its aesthetic qualities carry it beyond the memorial chores of archeology. To commemorate a culture, literature must present a unified vision in which the contradictions of history disappear or find poetic equivalents, and it is a small wonder that critics from antiquity onwards have seen the epics as both celebrations and encyclopedias. In the Middle Ages, elegies like the Old English *Wanderer* and *Seafarer* view a heroic society from the standpoint of a man driven to the fringes. As in *Deor,* cold objectifies the misery of banishment and symbolizes the stilled vista before recollection. The Wanderer's icy cold sea (*hrimcealde sæ*) is the path of exile (*wræclastas*), just as the Seafarer's winter on the ice cold sea (*iscealdne sæ*) gains a space of perception otherwise inaccessible to the man who enjoys prosperity on land. Nor is the isolation merely spacial and geographic. The Wanderer is a lone dweller (*anhaga*), while the Seafarer is deprived of kinsmen (*winemægum bidroren*). For the latter, his delight in nature points up this isolation, as the cries of seabirds replace the laughter of men in meadhalls.[23]

From their places outside homeland and community, the two speakers can define with particular clarity the role and behavior of individuals within a unified social order. The demands of a heroic life shared with kinsmen or pursued in isolation assume coherence as the speakers view them from a distance. The Wanderer makes it clear that such perspective is also an aspect of memory: his separation from the comfort of friends extends to an exile in time. Now cut off from the promises of treasure and intimacy, he sees that the imperatives of maintaining one's own wisdom and good counsel balance his former reliance on a lord occupying the gift throne. What he ascribes to this beloved protector (*leofra geholena*) is the guarantee of stability based not only on fealty but something approaching filial devotion. His thought projects an icon of authority, dependence, and submission:

> þinceð him on mode   þæt he his mondryhten
> clyppe ond cysse   ond on cneo lecge
> honda ond heafod,   swa he hwilum ær
> in geardagum   giefstolas breac.[24]

(He thinks in his mind that he clasps and kisses his man-lord and lays his hands and head on his knees, as when before in days past he enjoyed the gift-throne.)

The temporality of this vision betrays its deeper tensions. For the antithesis to these idealized heroic bonds follows the scene immediately in the speaker's waking state where dark waves, sea birds, and snow mixed with hail fill his actual sight. The contrast joins the Wanderer imaginatively to a community of warriors and kinsmen greeted by his music. And their swimming away into unknown songs returns him to a state of perception where, as in a poem like *The Ruin,* destroyed buildings image the wreckage of society and culture and their replacement by enigmatic monuments and hieroglyphs.

The Seafarer's exile also colors the transformations of memory, but without revising the underlying themes or the motifs that give them expression. Here the speaker's willingness to test the seas and seek the homes of foreigners *(elþeodigra eard)* differs from the Wanderer's enforced separation and calls to mind the earlier distinctions between necessary and willed exile in the wanderings of Aeneas. Cities and the landscape of the periphery entice him, yet he feels longing and his heart goes on hungry and greedy *(gifre ond grædig)*. From the testing occasioned by his journeys he learns to curb a violent mind and maintain trust, much as the other speaker exhorts his audience to keep private counsel and bear the oppression of sorrow in private thoughts. The poetic stress on temporality, carried out in *The Wanderer* by the *ubi sunt* motif, here builds from a sense of personal loss into a recognition of life's transience. In this expansion, memory acquires new boundaries as heroic deeds become spiritual battles against the devil, and the praise of men continues as unending praise with the angels.

A second mode of poetic transformation occurs in the creation of a parallel society from exile. This change deals with a narrative here and now, and within it lies an impulse toward restoration instead of predicament. Whether a second world or underground kingdom, the society created from exile attempts to rediscover and enact the values that are presumed to have governed the original order from which it has been expelled. Exile may resemble emigration, though a complete narrative often involves an eventual reintegration of the old and new social structures. In medieval literature, this mode of transformation seems to align itself with the chanson de geste and romance, just as the transformations of memory appear in the heroic elegy. The French cycle depicting baronial revolt against Charlemagne and Louis relates exiles to rival institutions. Girard de Roussillon leaves an inherited kingdom when Charlemagne demands allegiance of him. Renaud de Montauban in *Les Quatre Fils Aymon* is hounded by the emperor when he creates alternate kingdoms in Bordeaux and Galicia. Isembard converts to a Saracen faith in his exile and leads an army back to France against Louis. Courtly romance portrays kingdoms in the wasteland outside the court that rival King Arthur's chivalric order. Indeed, one can see in the *Morte d'Artur* that Lancelot's removing Guinevere to Joyous Garde represents an effort to reassert the values of the Round Table (now proved untenable) in a new setting when political collapse threatens. Perhaps the clearest illustration of how exile generates a parallel society and defines self may be found in the twelfth-century *Poema de Mio Cid* and related texts, which record Ruy Díaz's banishment and his efforts to form a new kingdom beyond Christian territory.

Scholars since Ramón Menéndez Pidal have insisted that medieval Spanish epic rests on the dual foundation of historical record and poetic metaphor. So it is hardly surprising to discover competing sources of explanation for the Cid's exile, though the connections among history, chronicles, ballads, and epics are often more confusing than Menéndez Pidal cared to admit.[25] In the ballad "En Santa Gadea de Burgos" and perhaps in the lost *Cantar de Sancho II y el cerco de Zamora,* the Cid's loyalty to King Sancho II and his public challenge to Alfonso VI after Sancho's death give cause for the new sovereign's wrath; the Cid's resentment of the court nobles and his military adventures help to sustain the enmity.[26] In other texts, the account is much more complicated yet no less adequate. Although the first leaf of Per Abat's manuscript of the *Poema de Mio Cid* is missing, the *Crónica de Veinte Reyes* portrays the Cid as a royal agent sent to collect tribute from the Moorish kings who rule Seville and Granada. With the aid of landed Christian magnates (*ricos omnes*) like García Ordóñez, the latter, Almudafar of Granada, has attacked Seville, threatening the peace and the king's ultimate authority. When the attackers ignore Ruy Díaz's courteous letters reminding them of obligations to the king, he gathers a force of Christians and Moors, wins a decisive battle, and takes prisoners, among them García Ordóñez whose beard he plucks as a sign of disrespect. After his men gather booty on the field, the Cid returns the rightful property to Almutamiz of Seville and allows the vassals of the Moorish king to take what they wish. Alfonso receives his tribute, but despite praising the Cid's deeds, soon accedes to the wishes of those who malign the hero. He sends letters granting the Cid nine days' grace to leave the kingdom of Castile.

These accounts contain the elements of a comprehensive economic myth that the poem develops.[27] Beneath the conflicts based on character and privilege are fundamental concerns with property and distribution. The cultural differences between Christians and Moors support a two-level economy which depends on internal regulation and external expansion— that is, on bureaucracy and imperialism. In the chronicle, the Cid appears first in the governmental role of an agent collecting revenues. The Christian noblemen who side with Almudafar represent traditional wealth, and they employ the mechanism of pillage to augment their positions as landholders. What they fail to recognize is that the balance of homeland and frontier is not equal and that territorial expansion can become a policy of central authority rather than the direct prerogative of an hereditary class. The chronicle emphasizes these differing recognitions by showing the Cid's using plunder to reward his own troops and the Moors loyal to Almutamiz, while returning to Alfonso his proper tribute. The vocabulary reveals these economic concerns by reference to *parias* ("tribute"), *debdo* ("debt"), *averes* ("possessions"), *riquezas* ("riches"), and *dones* ("gifts"). Describing the king's initial satisfaction with the Cid's action, the poem echoes similar language: "Fue muy pagado de quanto allá fiziera" ("He approved of what he did there"). After the decree of banishment, Álvar Fáñez pledges the retainers' loyalty to the Cid "como leales vassallos" willing to share possessions, property, and land: "Convusco despenderemos las mulas e los cavallos / e los averes e los paños" ("We shall share with you the mules and the horses and possessions and clothes" [serie 1]).[28]

The economic cast of these passages gives the Cid's exile a particular character that at once distinguishes it from other medieval examples and suggests new configurations. Unlike the Wanderer, the Cid evidences no grief over losing Alfonso as his lord; such sorrow would have appeared in the lost epic with Sancho's murder at Zamora before the poem opens. Accordingly, the Cid retains a sense of identity stemming not from a filial dependence or the reinforcement of companions but from public roles and actions he carries on independently, as in his continuing to be the king's agent. His distress on leaving his holdings at Vivar is a response to seeing the emptiness of "palacios yermos e desheredados" ("deserted and uninhabited palaces") and not a meditation on ruins from a lost culture. The poem's stylistic insistence on vacancy counterpoints the earlier thematic focus on gifts and prosperity: "Vío puertas abiertas e uços sin cañados, / alcándaras vázias sin pielles e sin mantos / e sin falcones e sin adtores mudados" ("He saw the open doors and gates without locks, poles without hides and cloaks and without falcons and molted birds" [3–5]). But unlike the Anglo-Saxon exiles, the Cid has a means of restoration. In the chronicle his battle with Almudafar and García Ordóñez has gained him a title—Campeador, "battler"—which identifies the way to compensate for loss through conquest. In the poem, his sight of the empty palace balances his pledge to return to Castile "a grand ondra" ("in great honor"). In succeeding episodes of the poem, the figurative terms that designate personal values, words like *bien* ("good"), *ondra* ("honor"), and *verdad* ("truth"), acquire economic associations and significance.

The Cid's exile has the rare advantage in medieval literature of financial subscription, and the success he enjoys in conquest resembles the yield on an investment. Deprived of fixed property by the king's letters, he turns immediately to sources where assets can be converted to cash and credit can be extended against his holdings. The contract which Martín Antolínez negotiates for him with the Jewish moneylenders Raquel and Vidas places the Cid's banishment in the context of a rudimentary mercantile system. The economic standard is not based on intrinsically valuable objects, although Raquel and Vidas believe they are holding valuable objects, but on a process of quantification (*notar, contar*) and credit. Two weighty chests filled with sand but said to carry gold represent the economic worth of inheritance, land, and recent booty. In Burgos the merchants carefully assess the overall worth of the Cid's assets (serie 9). Against this security they lend six hundred marks which Martín Antolínez accepts at the face value of currency, counting the silver and gold but not bothering to weigh the coins themselves (185). Their promise in return not to open the chests for a year reflects the governing principle in a credit economy that a breach of faith becomes a breach of contract, while honoring face value leads to dividends and even an agent's commission. The men who follow the Cid likewise abandon traditional standards of worth for measurements that promise increase. The Cid pledges to these one hundred fifteen kings in Burgos: "Vos, que por mí dexades casas e heredades, / enantes que yo muera, algún bien vos pueda far: / lo que perdedes doblado vos lo cobrar" ("To you who have left houses and inheritances for me, some good can befall before I die: what you lose will repay you double" [301–3]). On a spiritual plane, his vows to the monastery of San Pedro de Cardeña and to the Virgin continue the theme of economic investment by obligating him to good works as the return expected for grace.

The poem's economic theme connects as well with the mythic structure of center and periphery. The settled, hereditary order of Castile and León presents a locus of fixed values where honor, wealth, and power operate in scarcity and so require redistribution for social change to occur. Across the frontier and in an alien culture the Cid finds abundance and multiplication. His selling the captured fortress of Alcocer back to the Moors (serie 44) demonstrates a principle of economic fertility that stands out by contrast when natural attributes such as food and water are lacking and the land itself is sterile (838). The geography of exile permits new configurations as the Cid changes roles from an agent who regulates established values to a lord who generates new wealth: "qué bien pago a sos vassallos mismos! / A cavalleros e a peones fechos los ha ricos, / en todos los sos non fallariedes un mesquino" ("How well he rewarded his own vassals! He has made the knights and the foot soldiers rich; in all his men you would not find a poor man" [847–49]). As in the "liminal" phase in which a new personality arises, the social structures also take new form in a community of warriors and in service to Moorish rulers. By sending gifts to Alfonso throughout this period, the Cid maintains the relations of center and periphery, but at the same time his choosing to honor the king establishes an equivalence beween the two orders. When the Cid gains his kingdom in Valencia, reintegration can begin, as the old and new societies join in the king's marriage of the

Cid's daughters to the Infantes de Carrión and later in their resolving the Cid's grievance at the Infantes' mistreatment of his daughters through a common justice and second marriages.

The two modes of transformation that I have been describing—memory and an alternate society—connect exile to the past and present, respectively. A third mode avoids this determinism by projecting toward the future through the experience of imagination. We can see this development in the perspective that Dante gains on his own banishment from Florence. In the *Convivio* (1.3) he characterizes the "unjust punishment of exile and poverty": "After it was the pleasure of the citizens of that fairest and most famous daughter of Rome, Florence, to cast me out of her dearest bosom (wherein I was born and brought up to the summit of my life, and wherein with their good leave I desire with all my heart to rest my weary mind, and to end my allotted span), I have wandered through almost every region to which this tongue of ours extends, a stranger, almost a beggar, exposing to view against my will the stroke of fortune which is often wont unjustly to be charged to the account of the stricken."[29] Before long, his banishment with the Whites and Ghibellines carries into a second break, as he abandons the defeated faction and constitutes "a party by himself," a voluntary exile from the community of expatriots. His letters in support of Henry VII and the optimism within the *Purgatorio* reflect the promise of an earthly reconciliation in the establishment of imperial authority to complement ecclesiastical power in spiritual matters. Yet Henry's sudden death ends the prospect of revoking the sentences of death and banishment, and Dante's rejection of a degrading amnesty for himself (Epistula 12) confirms his separation. Accordingly, he has to look beyond mediating the secular and spiritual claims that prompt his exclusion and discover a larger synthesis of political reality within poetic truth.

The meetings with Brunetto Latini and Cacciaguida in the *Commedia* transform the nature of Dante's exile by locating his experience of the world in a vision where history and apocalypse meet. Brunetto's prophecy that both sides will seek to devour the poet because of his good deeds ("Per tuo ben far" [*Inferno* 15.64]) is at once immanent and already verified. Cacciaguida adds depth to these prophecies by viewing Dante within the continuities of lineage and descent and portraying Florence as it was in a Golden Age. The twin heritage of family and city reaches across the artificial divisions of time, affirming a sense of identity and fashioning civic concerns in their historical and moral dimensions. Free from "le cose contingenti" and gazing at "il punto / a cui tutti li tempi son presenti" ("The point to which all times are present" [*Paradiso*, 17.16–18]), Cacciaguida can tell Dante in plain language that he will be driven from Florence. The poem stresses that this fact of exile exists at the convergence of time: "Questo si vuole e questo già si cerca, / e tosto verrà fatto a chi ciò pensa" ("So is it willed, so already plotted, and so shall be accomplished soon by him who ponders upon it" [17.49–50]).[30] To Dante's fear that his poetry may lose him more than the place he holds dear Cacciaguida answers with a clear understanding of the moral and poetic mission of his isolation: "Tutta tua vision fa manifesta" (17.128).

The poet's numerous references in *Paradiso* to his faltering memory show that Dante's transformation of exile is something more than an elaborate retrospect in which the past is described as if it had not yet occurred and the narrator assumes a different perspective on fixed events. Rather, like Augustine (*Confessions* 11.21), Dante conceives time as it flows seamlessly toward him. He tells Cacciaguida, for example, "Ben veggio, padre mio, sì come sprona / lo tempio verso me" ("I see well, my father, how time spurs toward me" [17.106–7]). Thus what might seem fixed in memory is in fact part of a continuous process: future coming into the present and going into the past. But these boundaries of experience, joined within Providence, must be engaged in the here and now. For this reason, Dante as poet recurs to imagination not as a faculty subordinate to reason and memory but as an activity of mind where the historical reality of exile reveals its full meaning to a self still enmeshed in contingency.

Notes

1. *Sententiae* 158 in Otto Ribbeck, ed., *Scaenicae Romanorum poesis fragmenta* (1873; rpt. Hildesheim: George Olms, 1962), 2:323.

2. J. Wight Duff and Arnold M. Duff, trans., *Minor Latin Poets,* rev. ed., Loeb Classical Library (Cambridge: Harvard University Press, 1954), p. 39.

3. A. Ernout and A. Meillet, *Dictionnaire etymologique de la langue latine: Histoire des mots,* 4th ed. (Paris: C. Klinchsieck, 1959), p. 207.

4. Cf. Publilius, *Sententiae* 155: "Exsul, si tibi nusquam domus est, sine sepulcro es mortuus."

5. Penelope B. R. Doob, *Nebuchadnezzar's Children: Conventions of Madness in Middle English Literature* (New Haven: Yale University Press, 1974), pp. 54–94.

6. Cf. Matthew 16:24 and Luke 9:23, where *abneget* replaces *deneget. Biblia Sacra Vulgata,* ed. Robert Weber et al., 2 vols. (Stuttgart: Wurttenbergische Bibelanstalt, 1975).

7. Paul Tabori, *The Anatomy of Exile: A Semantic and Historical Study* (London: Harrap, 1972), pp. 43–45.

8. Theodor Mommsen, *Römisches Strafrecht* (1899, rpt., Darmstadt: Wissenschaftliche Buchgesellschaft, 1961), pp. 949, 957, 1010. James Leigh Strachan-Davidson, *Problems of the Roman Criminal Law,* 2 vols. (1912; rpt., Amsterdam: Editions Podopi, 1969), 2:23–74.

9. Herbert F. Jolowicz, *Historical Introduction to the Study of Roman Law,* 2d ed. (Cambridge: University Press, 1961), pp. 412–13.

10. *Lex Romana Burgundionum* 20, in *Fontes iuris Romani anteiustiniani,* ed. S. Riccobono et al., 3 vols (1941–43; rpt., Florence: S. A. G. Barbera, 1964), 2:732.

11. *Digesta Iustiniani Augusti,* ed. Theodor Mommsen and Paul Krüger, 2 vols. (1870; rpt., Berlin: Weidmann, 1963), 2:859, citing Marcian.

12. Du Cange, *Glossarium ad scriptores mediae et infimae Latinitatis,* s.v. *exilium;* R. E. Latham, *Revised Medieval Latin Word-List from British and Irish Sources* (London: Oxford University Press, 1965), s.v. *exilium, exul.*

13. W. Meyer-Lübke, *Romanisches Etymologisches Wörterbuch* (Heidelberg: Carl Winter, 1935),

s.v. *exiliare, exilium;* Walther von Wartburg, *Französisches Etymologisches Wörterbuch* (1934; rpt., Tübingen: J. C. B. Mohr, 1949), s.v. *exiliare, exilium.*

14. Giuseppe Mazzotta, *Dante, Poet of the Desert: History and Allegory in the Divine Comedy* (Princeton: Princeton University Press, 1979), pp. 271–74.

15. R. S. Pine-Coffin, trans., *Confessions* (Baltimore: Penguin, 1961), p. 147.

16. Etienne Gilson, *The Mystical Theology of Saint Bernard,* trans. A. H. C. Downes (New York: Sheed and Ward, 1940), p. 58.

17. A. J. Gossage, "Plutarch," in *Latin Biography,* ed. T. A. Dorey (New York: Basic Books, 1967), p. 57.

18. Michelle Houdeville-Augier, "Le phénomène de l'exclusion dans l'épisode de la folie d'Yvain, le chevalier au lion," in *Exclus et systèmes d'exclusion dans la littérature et la civilisation médiévales,* Senefiance, no. 5 (Paris: Champion, 1978), pp. 331–43, connects organic collapse to social difference and a new life, while arguing for Yvain's undergoing penance and eventually rejoining society. An alternate view is that Yvain's madness and recovery merely repeat the contradictions within the narrative; see Robert Edwards, "The Problem of Closure in Chrétien's *Yvain,*" in *The Twelfth Century: Acts 2,* ed. Sandro Sticca and Bernard Levy (Binghamton: Center for Medieval and Early Renaissance Studies, 1975), pp. 119–29.

19. Victor Turner, "Betwixt and Between: The Liminal Period in *Rites de Passage,*" in *The Forest of Symbols* (Ithaca: Cornell University Press, 1967), p. 97. Turner, "Passages, Margins, and Poverty: Religious Symbols of Communitas," in *Drama, Fields, and Metaphors: Symbolic Action in Human Society* (Ithaca: Cornell University Press, 1974), pp. 231–71, distinguishes an exile who preserves links with the culture from a true outsider.

20. Albert Cook, *Myth and Language* (Bloomington: Indiana University Press, 1980), p. 19.

21. Betty Rose Nagle, *The Poetics of Exile: Program and Polemic in the "Tristia" and "Epistulae ex Ponto" of Ovid* (Brussels: Latomus, 1980), pp. 83–86.

22. The translation is from R. K. Gordon, *Anglo-Saxon Poetry* (New York: Dutton, 1964), pp. 68, 70.

23. Stanley Greenfield, "The Formulaic Expression of the Theme of 'Exile' in Anglo-Saxon Poetry," *Speculum* 30 (1955): 200–6, rpt. in *Essential Articles for the study of Old English Poetry,* ed. Jess B. Bessinger, Jr. and Stanley J. Kahrl (Hamden, Connecticut: Archon Books, 1968), pp. 352–62, argues for a general stylistic consistency in the elegies.

24. Text in *The Exeter Book,* ed. George Philip Krapp and Elliott Van Kirk Dobbie, Anglo-Saxon Poetic Records, no. 3 (New York: Columbia University Press, 1936), p. 135. Translation mine.

25. For discussion, see Colin Smith, ed., *Poema de mio Cid* (Oxford: Clarendon Press, 1972), pp. xix–xxxvii. I am grateful to Philip Gericke for his suggestions on revising this section.

26. C. Colin Smith, *Spanish Ballads* (New York: Pergamon Press, 1964), pp. 96–99.

27. Julio Rodríguez Puértolas, "Un aspecto olvidado en el realismo del *Poema de Mio Cid,*" *PMLA* 82 (1967): 170–77; rpt. in *De la Edad Media a la edad conflictiva: estudios de literatura española* (Madrid: Gredos, 1972), pp. 169–87; and "El 'Poema de Mio Cid': nueva épica y nueva propaganda," in *"Mio Cid" Studies,* ed. A. D. Deyermond (London: Tamesis, 1977), pp. 141–59, connects the poem's artistic realism to a concern with material conditions.

28. *Cantar de Mio Cid,* ed. Ramón Menéndez Pidal, 3d ed., 3 vols. (Madrid: Espasa-Calpe, 1954), 2:1025.

29. W. W. Jackson, trans., *Dante's Convivio* (Oxford: Clarendon Press, 1909), p. 38.

30. *Paradiso,* trans. Charles S. Singleton, in *The Divine Comedy of Dante Alighieri,* 3 vols., Bollingen Series, no. 80 (Princeton: Princeton University Press, 1975).

Exile as Salvation in Hrotswitha's *Paphnutius*

SANDRO STICCA

In the history of eastern and western Christianity, the concept of exile is one of the most fundamental spiritual themes, particularly within the tradition of monasticism. The realization of *anachoresis,* the state of total physical and spiritual solitude, was deemed possible only by means of the *singularis eremi pugna,* that is, by the complete removal of the self from society to the perfect solitude of the *eremum,* the hermitage, to achieve spiritual progress and contemplative union with God. Whereas in ancient monasticism the desire for spiritual solitude, for personal exile from the world, was generally freely sought—either as an intense aspiration toward a higher degree of perfection or as means of a direct confrontation with the demonic temptations in order to refine the self through spiritual combat—solitary confinement or exile was at times specifically recommended or directly imposed on a sinner so that, through physical renunciation and penitential mortification of the flesh, he or she would be cleansed of worldly attachments and be spiritually reborn.

This kind of penitential exile was deemed particularly effective by Hrotswitha of Gandersheim, as can be seen in the articulation of two of her dramatic compositions: *Abraham* and *Paphnutius.* But while in the play of *Abraham* the salvific effect of solitude and exile are brought about by the holy hermit Abraham with gentle instructive forcefulness designed to bring the sinner Maria back into a state of grace, the regenerative and redemptive salvation of the prostitute Thais in *Paphnutius* is achieved by the hermit Paphnutius through the application of an unusually harsh and rigorous temporal exile, which is intended to test to the limits the human frailty and will power of Thais. Indeed, Paphnutius's austere resolve to rescue Thais from her sinful life and bring her back on the road to salvation by subjecting her to a violent maceration of the flesh has been looked upon by some early critics as an illustration of the hermit's inflexible and inhuman monastic vigor. In 1868, for instance, Elie Petit, in one of the earliest critical readings of Hrotswitha's work, observed that to achieve Thais's salvation, the hermit

Paphnutius strikes the thunder of reprobation without any discretion whatever: "Paphnuce fait entendre . . . pour sauver Thaïs, le tonnerre de la réprobation,"[1] and Rigobon remarks that Paphnutius resembles a pitiless judge more than a minister of divine justice as he directs that Thais be shut up in a narrow cell to initiate her penance.[2] Modern scholarship, on the other hand, has stressed the fact that in the play Paphnutius's imposition of an extremely rigid form of penance is counterbalanced by his display of a solemn and moving commotion at the end of the play while he comforts the repentant and dying Thais.[3]

The basic concern of this study will be primarily to show how, in the play of *Paphnutius,* the motif of the exile from the world imposed as an austere form of penance is used as a vehicle to intensify Thais's struggle toward her spiritual redemption and to develop and resolve the dramatic conflict at the religious and aesthetic level. Although as I have had occasion to observe, in the play of *Abraham,* the sanctification of the sinner Mary is achieved by the hermit Abraham in a gentler fashion because of the ties of kinship they share[4]—she is in fact his niece—the more energetic and inflexible kind of penitential exile imposed on the harlot Thais is the result not so much of the hermit Paphnutius's more intransigent character but rather the intensely sinful nature of a situation that demanded the application of a radical spiritual remedy.[5] The justification for this harsh measure is provided by Paphnutius himself, when having brought Thais to the convent to be walled in a narrow cell, he tells the abbess that she who had sinned in the world must now be secluded from it:

> But since the sickness of the body, like that of the soul, must be cured by the medicine of contraries, it follows that she must be sequestered from the tumult of worldly temptations into a narrow cell, so that she may contemplate alone and undisturbed her sins.[6]

As in Hrotswitha's other plays, the thematic structure of *Paphnutius* is framed within the larger and more complex dimensions of Christian doctrine and thought, in particular the incessant struggle between good and evil and the constant temporal preoccupation of the faithful with attaining a further stage of perfection and realizing their potential for sanctification. The prefatory *argumentum* succinctly resumes the play's fundamental actions: Thais's rescue from the brothel by Paphnutius, her confinement to a narrow cell for five full years to accomplish her penance, and her death in Christ fifteen days later:

> Conversio Thaidis meretricis quam Pafnutius heremita, aeque ut Habraham, sub specie adiens amatoris convertit et, data poenitentia, per quinquennium in augusta cellula conclusit, donec, digna satisfactione deo reconciliata, XVa peractae poenitentiae die obdormivit in Christo.[7]

(The conversion of Thais the harlot whom the hermit Paphnutius converted, as Abraham before, disguised as a lover. After giving her a
penance, he confined her to a narrow cell for five years, until reconciled to
God through a worthy penance, fifteen days thereafter she died in Christ).

The plot of the play is characterized by the simplicity of its structural
components. Directed by a vision, the hermit Paphnutius leaves the desert
and disguised as a lover, seeks out Thais in a brothel; he moves her to
repentance, and after a five-year penance in a narrow cell she is reconciled
with God; fifteen days after her penance is accomplished she dies in the
Lord. Although a critical interpretation of the play can be based solely on
the "careful thematic linkage"[8] and on obvious "harmonies of theme and
structure"[9] that Hrotswitha was able to weave in her plays, a full understanding of Thais's striving for moral perfection can only be attained
through an analysis of the hagiographical and monastic context upon which
the play is grafted. Indeed, although in the composing of all her dramas
Hrotswitha drew on that vast collection of hagiographical material known
as the *Vitae Patrum*,[10] it is especially in her two most perfect artistic creations, *Abraham* and *Paphnutius,* that the conversion of the harlots Mary and
Thais is brought about by the personal perfection and sanctity of holy
hermits. Before analyzing the theme of the exile in the play, therefore, the
reader must first be aware of the hagiographical tradition within which the
dramatic action is articulated and then recognize the distinct contemporary
consuetudo monastica (monastic custom) of which this play is a genuine
expression.
    That Hrotswitha found the sources of her dramatic production in
hagiography today is unquestioned among medieval scholars.[11] For our
immediate purposes, however, it is necessary to elucidate the reason for
Hrotswitha's choice of stories taken from the literature of the ancient fathers
of monasticism. The answer can be found in the fact that medieval exegetical tradition looked upon martyrdom and monastic life as the clearest
manifestations of the Christian ideal. Particularly in the early years of the
Christian era, martyrdom was regarded as the perfect imitation of Christ.
Tertullian, for example, states that the title of martyr is attained through
one's death for Christ: "Proprie enim martyribus nihil iam reputari potest,
quibus in lavacro ipsa vita deponitur" ("Nothing in fact can be still considered particular about the martyrs if not the fact that they lay down their life
in blood"),[12] and Origen affirms that only those are called true martyrs
who suffer death for the faith: "Only those who fought even unto death for
truth and strength are traditionally referred to as martyrs."[13]
    With the end of the persecutions, however, when the possibility no longer
existed for physical martyrdom, it is in the ascetic life, hermitic and monastic, that Christianity finds the perfect example of the *imitatio Christi* (imita-

tion of Christ).[14] Monastic life comes to be looked upon in patristic spirituality as the best exemplification of spiritual martyrdom in times of peace and tranquility; the monk becomes the new "martyr" offering proof of his love for Christ through a continuous form of martyrdom based on renunciation, self-denial, mortification, and abnegation. St. John Chrysostom, for instance, recommends the mortification and crucifixion of one's body if one wishes to receive the crown of martyrdom: "Corpus tuum morte affice et crucifige, et ipse quoque accipies coronam martirii" ("Punish and crucify your body with death and you shall receive the crown of martyrdom").[15]

But if cenobitic life with its ideal of renunciation of the world and mortification of the body was considered to be a prolongation and extension of martyrdom, it is more specifically hermitic life that is regarded as the highest and most sublime manifestation of monastic life. The vigor and deprivation associated with the penitential life of the hermit were often summarized in the expression: "Parcus in cibo, parcus in lecto, parcus in somnno" ("Moderate in food, moderate in bed, moderate in sleep").[16] Hermitic life, marked by the rigor of its *solitudo* (solitude), was esteemed to be a constant *colluctatio* (struggle), a *certamen* (fight) against the temptations of the devil: "Only solitude allows man to discover, and therefore to confront, all the obscure forces that he carries within himself. . . . Solitude is a terrible trial, for it makes crack and burst the veneer of our superficial securities."[17] With good reason, therefore, in monastic tradition the hermit was considered, to employ the terminology of Delaruelle, "le héros du monastère" ("the hero of the monastery").[18] Recognizing that martyrdom and hermitic life constituted in patristic times the two privileged aspects of the Christian ideal of life, Hrotswitha, in her dramas *Abraham* and *Paphnutius,* tried to illustrate the notion that "hermitic life is, like martyrdom, a way of practicing the imitation of Christ to the utmost, because perfect solitude is that which requires the greatest renunciation and, finally, despite appearances, the greatest love."[19] Having offered in the plays of *Dulcitius, Gallicanus, Callimachus* and *Sapientia* a celebration of martyrdom, she turned in *Abraham* and *Paphnutius* to the celebration of hermitic life because it also constituted one of the most popular practices of tenth-century monasticism.[20]

At the beginning of *Paphnutius,* Hrotswitha introduces the essential spiritual concern of the hermit Paphnutius by articulating it within the eternally harmonious rapport that ought to exist in God's universally ordered harmony between macrocosm and microcosm. As Paphnutius's attentive and solicitous disciples inquire about the cause of his somber and grieved countenance, the hermit replies that his sadness is the result of an injury inflicted on God; and when the disciples wish to know the nature of the injury the hermit explains that it is an injury inflicted on the Creator by His own creature, whom He created in His own image: "Ipsam, quam a propria patitur creatura ad sui imaginem condita."[21] Whereupon Paphnutius plunges into a disquisition on the harmonious music by means of which God governs the universe. Hrotswitha's insertion of a prefatory musicological discussion into the structure of the play has been considered by some critics either as thematically irrelevant or as metaphysically ungraspable. Others still have justified this intrusion by observing that Hrotswitha was indulging in the traditional medieval desire to exhibit one's learning. Kronenberg, for example, points out that particularly in her last two plays, *Abraham* and *Paphnutius,* Hrotswitha was trying to show both her erudition and writing skills: "Sie erwies sich als *Magistra artium liberalium*—Meisterin der freien Künste" ("She proved herself to be *Magistra artium liberalium*—a master of liberal arts").[22] Recent critics, however, have recognized the essential metaphorical function performed by the musical preface in the architectural totality of the play. Chamberlain, in particular, has illustrated the specific role of musical imagery in *Paphnutius* by demonstrating its relevance in the play to moral action and edification.[23] Paphnutius's discussion on music has a fundamental theological function; it is designed to make the numinous intelligible to his disciples. As part of the quadrivium, music played an important role in evoking the vision of the harmony that binds the microcosm to the macrocosm and, therefore, man to God: "In Hrotswitha's time the four teaching divisions of the Quadrivium served in the end only this purpose, to bring the Microcosmos in harmony with the Macrocosmos, that is to lead men to God."[24] Spitzer too, for instance, has shown to what an extent "the idea of world harmony, in which music is seen as symbolizing the totality of the world, is an idea which was ever present to the mind of the Middle Ages."[25] It is in the light of these considerations that one realizes the structural significance and importance of music in *Paphnutius* and the necessity of understanding the hierarchical function of the musical metaphor in the play's interpretation.

In the play, Paphnutius is particularly distressed because God's universally ordered harmony is disturbed by a discordant note, which arbitrarily and capriciously has isolated itself from the harmonious unity of the world. Unable to comprehend the ethical import of Paphnutius's musicological elaboration, the disciples ask him to more clearly identify the cause of his sadness, to which he abruptly replies: "Quaedam impudens femina moratur in hac patria" ("A certain shameless woman dwells in this land")[26] and immediately proceeds to identify the woman: "Thais." Thais is the beautiful discordant note: "Haec miranda praenitet pulchritudine et horrenda sordet turpitudine" ("She shines forth with her beauty but is filthy in her foul turpitude)".[27] The musicological opening of the play, when seen within this perspective, assumes artistic and structural validity within the dramatic whole. In fact, the musicological discussion constitutes the framework within which the dramatic action will move toward its resolution; for the *discordia* present in God's harmonious world will be resolved at the end of the play into *concordia,* when Thais, regenerated, will no longer upset the universally ordered harmony. The musicological framework that governs the play is intrinsically connected in temporal terms with the concept of exile, for the *discordia* that Thais has caused by freely choosing to exile herself from God's world will be turned into a *concordia* when she will accept the exile from her sinful world that will be imposed on her by the hermit Paphnutius. Since, according to St. Augustine, "Vice in the soul arises from its own doing,"[28] Thais's sin constitutes an *exile,* an *alienation* from God reflecting St. Paul's assertion that the state of sin is an estrangement from God: "Since you were at that time without Christ, you were exiled."[29] The harmonious rapport to be achieved between the macrocosm and the microcosm is therefore by extension a paradigmatic exemplification of the harmonious order to be achieved by Thais; for only after overcoming the internal and external discord within herself caused by her sinful condition can she be finally reunited spiritually with God. Paphnutius's discourse in the first scene of the play makes it amply clear that Thais is a dissonance introduced in God's harmonious world, a dissonance that threatens not only her own salvation but that of many people as well through temptation:

. . . non dignatur cum paucis ad interitum tendere, sed prompta est omnes lenociniis suae formae illicere secumque ad interitum trahere.[30]

(Not satisfied with leading a few men to eternal damnation she is ready to drag along with her all men to damnation through the allurement of her beauty).

Once the moral dissonance has been identified in God's world, Paphnutius, in a crescendo of scriptural references and allusions, initiates the salvific movement designed to redeem Thais. Fearing that he would not be received by her as a hermit, he decides to visit Thais disguised as a lover and in the process risks his own salvation, for as he tells his disciples before leaving: "Fulcite me interim precibus assiduis ne superer insidiis vitiosi serpentis" ("Support me all the while with your constant prayers so that I shall not be overcome by the temptations of the vicious serpent").[31] Fully cognizant of the spiritual dangers attendant upon Paphnutius's imminent confrontation with Satan, his disciples reply: "Qui regem prostravit tenebricolarum, largiatur tibi contra hostem triumphum" ("May He Who overcame the prince of darkness grant you triumph over the enemy").[32]

The meeting between the harlot and the hermit in scene 3 is artistically effective, for although the play propounds two basic theological theses—that salvation can come only from God and that man must turn toward Him and open his heart to His grace—Hrotswitha renders the narrative intelligible and credible by having the drama of sin and salvation resolved in a direct confrontation between Thais and Paphnutius. Hrotswitha frames the meeting between the two within a metaphorical language that in its rich spiritual symbolism reinforces Thais's perception of true love in her movement from carnal to divine love. When Paphnutius disguised as a lover enters the brothel, he tells Thais he is "amator tuus" ("your lover");[33] Hrotswitha, however, brings to full development the fundamentally carnal meaning of that phrase through its contextual juxtaposition, later in the play, when salvation has been accomplished, with the words "pater tuus" ("your father") and "dilectione" ("spiritual love").[34] Although Thais has taken many lovers before, Paphnutius is the only one who loves her truly, who cares for her soul. As Thais promptly replies that "Quicumque me amore colit, aequam vicem amoris a me recepit" ("Whoever seeks me in love, finds me returning his love"),[35] it is obvious that she is bound to react positively to Paphnutius's vivifying salvific act, which in itself represents the full blossoming of the sacramental expression of God's saving act of love. Although Thais knows how to love, she does not know what to love; she does not know proper love. Paphnutius, however, is not an "amator" but a "dilector." In strict Augustinian tradition,[36] Hrotswitha uses the term *amor* for love of the physical kind, the word *dilectio* for a high-minded spiritual love, and the verb *diligere,* generally, for the act of charitable loving. Paphnutius, like Christ, is a true lover. He has proven the quality of his love; by facing the temptations of the brothel, he has risked the salvation of his own soul. Paphnutius's action is an expression of the divine love and power, and thus at the end of the encounter Thais rises, ready to achieve a definitive transition from the fallen state to a new life in God.

Thais's movement toward justification and grace cannot be accomplished, however, unless it first be preceded by a twofold renunciation: namely, the way of the World with its possessions, and the way of the Flesh with its carnal pleasures, her lovers. Indeed, when Thais asks the holy hermit how she can best effect the gift of reconciliation and forgiveness, Paphnutius immediately replies: "Contempne saeculum, fuge lascivorum consortia amasionum."[37] The road to salvation entails a complete abjuring of the world: "Show contempt for the world and flee the company of your lascivious lovers."

Since Thais's riches have been generated by the fire of passion she instilled in her lovers, it is just and proper that her wealth be burned publicly in their presence. The symbolism is evident; the group of young men who provided Paphnutius with information about the whereabouts of Thais had referred to her at the beginning of the play with the words, "Ipsa nostratium est ignis" ("She is our very own fire").[38] Exegetical tradition often interprets the term *ignis* symbolically as *luxuria* and *concupiscentia;*[39] Alanus de Insulis in his *Sermo in Die Cinerum,* after having identified the fire of wrath, the fire of luxury, and the fire of avarice as the triple forerunner of the infernal fires, suggests that the proper way to extinguish the fire of concupiscence is by eliminating the object that engenders it: "Let also the object of luxury be eliminated so that the mind shall not desire vain things nor shall the emotion stray away into frivolous things."[40] And this is precisely what Thais does; she burns all her wealth "so that no longer will remain in the world the things that I have acquired through evil, wronging the Creator of the world."[41] The road to salvation is now open; as Thais joyfully returns to announce to Paphnutius that she has disposed of her worldly possessions— "res familiares disposui"—and publicly denounces her lovers, "meis amasionibus abrenuntiavi," the hermit exclaims in spiritual exultation: "Quia his abrenuntiasti, superno amatori iam nunc poteris copulari" ("Since you have abandoned them, you will now be able to enjoy the embraces of the Heavenly Bridegroom").[42] By renouncing all mundane concerns Thais will now be able to enjoy the embrace of her heavenly lover, Christ. Scene 5 culminats in Thais's total surrender to the spiritual care of Paphnutius, whom she beseeches to be a lantern to her, a *radius,* a sparkle of divine light, a scintilla of heavenly fire leading her out of the darkness of sin.

The process of ethical and moral reorientation, the transition from the mundane to the spiritual, is immediately initiated when Paphnutius fittingly leads Thais from the brothel to the monastery, "sacrarum virginum nobile . . . collegium" ("a noble company of holy virgins"),[43] where she will undertake her five years' penance for her sins against purity. The entire episode of Thais's penance deserves particular analysis not only because it offers the clearest illustration of the theme of exile but also because it provides distinct insights into Hrotswitha's ability to express within the pattern of dramatic action contemporary practices and monastic and hermitic concerns. It is with a scriptural allusion, that of the shepherd rescuing his sheep, that Paphnutius entrusts Thais to the care of the Abbess of the monastery in scene 7:

> Attuli capellam semivivam, dentibus luporum nuper abstractam, quam tui miserationi foveri, tui sollicitudine gestio mederi, quoadsque, abiecta haedinae pellis austeritate, ovini velleris induatur mollitie.[44]

> (I have brought you a half-dead little she goat, recently torn from the teeth of the wolves. I hope that by your compassion it shall have shelter, and through your care, it shall be cured, until she shall have cast aside the rough pelt of a goat and be clothed with the soft wool of the lamb).

The discussion that ensues in the rest of the scene, first between the Abbess and Paphnutius and then between Thais and Paphnutius, unquestionably constitutes the focus of the dramatic action, the highlight of the play, for it identifies the monastic concern that *Paphnutius* was designed to illustrate. Before leaving Thais in the monastery to fulfill the penance, Paphnutius provides the Abbess with specific instructions as to *how* and *where* it should be conducted:

> Quia enim aegritudo animarum aeque ut corporum contrariis curanda est medelis, consequens est, ut haec, a solita saecularium inquietudine sequestrata, sola in augusta retrudatur cellula, quo liberius possit discutere sui crimina.[45]

> (Since the sickness of the body, like that of the soul, must be cured by the medicine of contraries, it follows that she must be sequestered from the tumult of wordly temptations into a narrow cell, so that she may contemplate alone and undisturbed her sins).

Although Thais's repentance could have logically and completely been accomplished within the sacred walls of the monastery, Paphnutius insists that she be shut up in a narrow cell: *Thais must be exiled* from the world. The importance of the word *cellula* (small cell) in the understanding of the play will become apparent both from our discussion and from the fact that it occurs in scene 7, which is the longest in the play and is dramatically located at its center. Paphnutius orders the Abbess to have a small cell built, "quantocius cellula construatur," with no entrance or exit whatever but a small window: "Nullus introitus, nullus relinquatur aditus, sed solummodo exigua fenestra."[46] Paphnutius brings to this task an almost single-minded determination, an ascetic and hermitic harshness and zeal; immediately after the cell is readied Paphnutius bids Thais to enter it: "Ingredere, Thais, habitaculum tuis facinoribus deflendis satis congruum" ("Enter, Thais, your cell, a proper place for deploring your sins").[47] As Thais, not yet tempered by penitential sacrifices, voices her concern that soon her cell will be uninhabitable to live in due to the smell generated by the needs of her bodily functions, Paphnutius unceremoniously answers that the purification of her body must be achieved through her own bodily filth: "Convenit, ut male blandientis dulcedinem delectationis luas molestia nimii foetoris" ("It is only right that you atone for the sinful sweetness of alluring delight by suffering this awful stink").[48] The scene ends as Paphnutius bids Thais to implore God's mercy while at the same time stressing the urgency of his own return to the hermit's cell.

The concept of exile from the world becomes even more meaningful in the light of the spiritual orientation by which Hrotswitha is governed. She is advocating a particularly rigorous temporal penance for Thais, which could only be accomplished within the starkly ascetic and severely restricting limits of a *cella*: total physical and mental exile. Although the medieval monastic spirituality of the tenth and eleventh centuries, particularly Benedictine asceticism, was characterized by two fundamental aspects, renunciation of pleasures and fight against temptations,[49] the question remained as to the most rigorous and best way to accomplish this spiritual combat. In choosing for this purpose hermitic life, and particularly the solitary con-finement of a cell, Hrotswitha was not only following, as we shall see, a *consuetudo monastica* that reflected contemporary practices in Germany, es-pecially Saxony, but also a general monastic tradition, which at this time considered hermitic life the highest level of religious life. In an illuminating essay on hermits in Germany from the tenth to the twelfth century, Herbert Grundmann indicates that during this period mention is made of several hermits—*inclusi* and *inclusae,* "Klausner" and "Klausnerinnen"—who did not live in the monastic community of the monastery but rather next to a convent or church in a rigorous individual claustration, walled in a cell—"Zelle or Klause"—that did not have any door but only a window through which food was provided.[50] This is a description that perfectly reflects what happens in the play of *Paphnutius;* as we have seen earlier, the hermit describes to the Abbess the specifications of the cell thus: "Nullus introitus, nullus relinquatur aditus, sed solummodo exigua fenestra, per quam modicum possit victum accipere" ("Leave no entrance nor exit, but just a narrow window through which she may receive a small quantity of food").[51] Thais thus becomes a "Klausnerin," segregated, exiled from the world to undertake the purgative preparation for her salvation.

There remains to be considered in the interpretation of the play the metaphorical meaning clearly associated with the words *cella* or *cellula,* and the function of the five-year penance assigned to Thais. Against the back-ground provided by this hermitic tradition and within the specific context offered by the play, it is easy to understand the prominence given the words *cella* and *cellula* if one but realizes that the *cella* was considered to be the most perfect *locus heremiticae conversationi,* the most suitable place to temper the soul, the arena of spiritual triumph, the gateway to heaven. The *cella* is the best place to exile Thais, for in it "the recluse became liturgically and psychologically dead to the world."[52] St. Peter Damian in his *Laus Eremiticae Vitae* provides perhaps the clearest and most elaborate commen-tary on hermitic life and on the word *cella:*

> Indeed, solitary life is the school of celestial doctrine and the discipline of divine arts. . . . Oh cell, store-room of celestial merchants . . . happy commerce where terrestrial things are exchanged for celestial ones and the transitory is changed into the eternal. . . . Oh cell, wondrous workshop of spiritual exercise, in which assuredly the human soul restores in itself the image of its Creator and regains its original purity! . . . Oh cell, tabernacle of sacred warfare . . . field of divine fight, arena of spiritual combat, stage of the angels, wrestling school for hard-fighting wrestlers, where the spirit engages in combat with the flesh.[53]

Significantly pertinent to our discussion is Damian's observation that it is in the cell, a wondrous workshop of spiritual exercise, that the human soul restores the image of its Creator and regains its original purity: "O cella spiritualis exercitii mirabilis officina, in qua certe humana anima Creatoris sui in se restaurat imaginem, et ad suae redit originis puritatem!"[54] Since at the beginning of the play Paphnutius had explained to his disciples that his sadness was caused by the injury inflicted on the Creator by a creature created *in His own image,* the harlot Thais, it is quite logical that she should be exiled in a cell where the restoration of God's image in her soul and the regaining of her original purity could be accomplished. The concluding sentence of the *Laus eremiticae vitae* offers a most dramatic crystallization of Paphnutius's specific purpose in confining Thais to a solitary life in a narrow cell:

> Qui singularem hanc vitam usque ad finem suae pro divino amore ten-
> uerit, de habitaculo carnis egressus, ad aedificationem ineffabilem per-
> veniet, domum non manufactam, aeternam in coelis.[55]

> (He who, for love of God, holds to this singular way of life until his death, having gone out from the dwelling of the flesh, shall reach the ineffable building, the not hand-made eternal abode in heaven).

The penitential martyrdom undertaken by Thais in her "exigua cellula" is ordained to be accomplished within a five-year period, which in medieval numerical exegesis is meant to express that the expiation of her sins is coordinated with the number five, a traditional symbol of man's senses and carnal sensuality. Isidore of Seville, for instance, writes that the number five symbolizes "sensus quoque corporis quinque, visus, auditus, odoratus, gustus et tactus" ("also the five senses of the body, sight, hearing, smell, taste and touch"),[56] and Hugh of St. Victor indicates that "quinque . . . humanae carnis sensualitas est . . . quinque vero sensus corporis" ("the number five . . . is the sensuality of the human flesh . . . indeed the five senses of the body").[57] The symbolical function of the number five is here quite clear; it is juxtaposed to the five penitential stages Thais must undergo before attaining her perfection and sanctification. Hugh of St. Victor identi-fies these five stages as: "Contritio in corde, confessio in ore, maceratio carnis, correctio in opere, perseverantia in virtute," that is, contrition of the heart, oral confession, maceration of the flesh, correction by means of works (spiritual) and perseverance in virtue.[58] And it is at the end of the five years of her penitential exile that Paphnutius leaves his own cell to visit the hermit Antony to urge him and his disciples to join him in continuous prayer until God provides a sign that Thais's repentant tears have merited for her His forgiveness. Her regeneration and purification are soon joyfully announced by Antony, and Paphnutius immediately sets out to visit her in her cell. The encounter in scene 12 between Paphnutius and Thais is meant to convey the epiphanic joy of God's efficacious sign of forgiveness. Whereas in scene 3, on visiting Thais in the brothel *sub specie amatoris,* disguised as a lover, he addressed her as *amator tuus,* he now speaks as *pater tuus,* her spiritual father; moreover, Thais's transfiguration is expressed in a rich flow of liturgical and biblical paraphrasing. As Thais despairs of salvation by indicating to the hermit that she has done nothing in the five years worthy of God, Paphnutius replies: "Si deus iniquitates observabit, nemo sustinebit" ("If God shall observe our iniquities, no one shall sustain us").[59] When after declining the hermit's gentle injunction to follow him out of her cell, Thais relents, in hopes that through her penance she has deserved to escape God's punishment, Paphnutius's reply is couched in Pauline words: "Gratuitum dei donum non pensat humanum meritum, quia, si meritis tribueretur, gratia non dicetur" ("The gratuitous gift of God is not concerned with human merit, for, if it were attributed to merits, it would not be called grace").[60] The scene ends as Thais, uplifted by the joy brought by Paphnutius's words, leaves the cell and bursts into a prayer of exultant thanksgiving:

Unde laudet illum caeli concentus omnisque terrae surculus, necnon universae animalis species atque confusae aquarum gurgites, quia non solum peccantes patitur, sed etiam poenitentibus praemia gratis largitur.[61]

(Therefore praise Him the harmonious company of heaven and all the little springs on earth, and all the living creatures and all the whirlpools of the waters in their fall, because He not only suffers those who sin but also rewards those who repent with the gift of grace).

The play's theophany occurs in the final scene, which in its comprehensive numerological conception and with Paphnutius's final speech restates the drama's fundamental concern by reintegrating Thais, the discordant note, into God's universal harmony after a five-year exile. Although the salvation of Thais has been foretold in scene 11 through the epiphanic vision experienced by Paul, Hrotswitha chose to have Thais's death and hence, her soul's ascent to heaven, occur fifteen days after she has been led away from her solitary cell by Paphnutius. The number fifteen is aptly chosen, for it provides a significant and pertinent commentary on the central theme of Thais's salvation. In fact, the number fifteen is emblematic of her salvation, for that number connotes eternal life. Isidore of Seville, for instance, states that the number fifteen is made up mystically of two constituent numbers, seven and eight, the former connoting temporal time, the latter eternal time; he further elaborates the distinction by indicating that just as by the number seven present life is designated, so too by the number eight the mystery of future eternal resurrection is manifested.[62] St. Augustine interprets the number eight as signifying judgment day; reaffirming the connection between the two numbers, he states that after the number seven, which symbolizes the passing of this life, comes the number eight, which signifies judgment day when holy people are transferred from temporal works to eternal life.[63] Even more pertinent to our analysis is the comment by Hugh of St. Victor, who interprets the numerical combination of the numbers of eight and seven as signifying eternity after mutability.[64] There is no doubt that Hrotswitha's intention was to provide in the juxtaposed gradational sequence of the two numbers an allegorical evocation and prefiguration of the salvation of Thais, who, after leaving her humanity and the temporal world for five years of exile in a cell, is now ready to meet her divine judge, the architect through the hermit Pahpnutius of her regeneration and salvation.

Paphnutius's speech at the end of the play extends and completes the symbolical complexity of this numerical allegoresis by supplicating God that the various parts of Thais, the temporal and the spiritual, made consubstantially whole again, be allowed to join the heavenly chorus and partake of the joys of the heavenly host:

> Qui factus a nullo, vere es sine materia forma . . . da diversas partes huius solvendae hominis prospere repretere principium sui originis, quo et anima caelitus indita, caelestibus gaudiis intermisceatur . . . haec Thais resurgat perfecta, ut fuit, homo, inter candidulas oves collocanda et in gaudium aeternitatis inducenda.[65]

> (Thou Who art uncreated, Thou Who art truly form without matter . . . grant that the dissolving, diverse parts of this human being may happily return to the source of its beginnings, so that its divinely infused soul may mingle with the celestial joys . . . that Thais be resurrected as perfect as before, a human being to be placed among the white lambs and led into the joy of eternal life).

Paphnutius's final speech, with its emphasis on the harmonious union of the spiritual with the physical in Thais constitutes, conceptually and dramatically, a return to the preoccupation that he expressed at the very beginning of the play to his disciples that a discordant note existed in their very midst that ran contrary to divine harmony. Not only was Thais a dissonant element in God's universe but the disharmony existed even within herself through the dissonance she had created between her body and her soul by her sinful life. Paphnutius, however, had also indicated that dissonant elements in proper combination can make one single world: "Dissona elementa, convenienter concordantia, unum perficiunt mundum."[66] Paphnutius's prayer at the end of the play seeks in its request for the complete unity of all dissonant parts of Thais to eliminate the original dissonance and achieve in the process that *discordia-concors* so dear to the medieval audience. That Hrotswitha should have articulated Thais's fall from and return to grace against the background of medieval musical concepts should not surprise us, since, as Spitzer has shown, the Middle Ages felt that "the harmony of the cosmos, like that of music, is a gift of grace."[67] Even more important in this context is Paphnutius's remark at the beginning of the play concerning the enormity of the injury or harm done to God by His own creature, Thais, whom He made in His very image. Paphnutius's fundamental request in the final prayer at the end of the play is precisely for the harmonious restoration of all dissonant parts of Thais so that she can seek once more the Source of her beginnings, her Creator: "Da diversas partes huius solvendae hominis prospere repetere principium sui originis."[68]

It would appear from our analysis of the play of *Paphnutius* that Hrotswitha was governed by a personal aesthetic vision that relied not only on the resources offered by contemporary interest in music, hermitic life, and exegetical numerology but also on her personal interpretation and expression of the material of the story that she found in hagiographical sources. Thais's internal dramatic conflict between carnal and spiritual forces remains reasonably characterized by a subtle interplay of divine and human elements, even at the play's highest moments of monastic fervor, religious edification, liturgical references, and scriptural exegesis. Within the obvious larger religious dimensions of the play, the character of Thais is illuminated by the distinct personal traits of her individuality, which rises, through moral responsibility, ethical perception of her sins and their expiation in exile, to the highest heroic plateau in the ladder of salvation and sanctification. The theme of exile, articulated within the parameters of Christian doctrine and monastic tradition, fulfills not only a religious and pedagogical function but an artistic one as well; for the feelings of distress and anguish felt by Thais when she is first shut up in her narrow cell are utterances that emanate from a soul not yet fortified by penance as it anticipates the suffering and misery to which she will be subject in her long and solitary confinement.

Notes

1. "Théâtre de Hrotswitha," *Revue de l'art chrétien* 12 (1868): 15.

2. Marcella Rigobon, *Il teatro e la latinità di Hrotswitha* (Florence: A. Milani, 1930), p. 6: "Rigido e inflessibile nell' imporre a Taide le penitenze più terribili, Pafnuzio assomiglia più ad uno spietato giudice che ad un ministro della divina carità" ("Rigid and inflexible in imposing the most terrible penances on Thais, Paphnutius resembles more a heartless judge than a minister of divine charity").

3. Ferruccio Bertini, *Il 'teatro' di Rosvita* (Gena: Tilgher, 1979), p. 71.

4. Sandro Sticca, "Hrotswitha's *Abraham* and Exegetical Tradition," *Saggi critici in onore di Vittorio D'Agostino* (Turin: Baccola and Gili, 1971), pp. 359–85, 368.

5. Bert Nagel, "The Dramas of Hrotsvit of Gandersheim," *The Medieval Drama and Its Claudelian Revival,* ed. E. Catherine Dunn, Tatiana Fotitich, and Bernard M. Peebles (Washington: Catholic University of America Press, 1970), p. 22; see also his *Hrotsvit von Gandersheim* (Stuttgart: J. B. Metzlersche Verlagsbuchhandlung, 1965), p. 59.

6. Paulus de Winterfeld, *Hrotsvithae Opera,* new ed. (Berolini: Apud Weidmannos, 1965), p. 174: "Quia enim aegritudo animarum aeque ut corporum contrariis curanda est medelis,

consequens est, ut haec, a solita saecularium inquietudine sequestrata, sola in angusta re-trudatur cellula, quo liberius possit discutere sui crimina." All subsequent citations from *Paphnutius* will be taken from De Winterfeld's edition.

7. Ibid., p. 162.

8. Katharina Wilson, *The Dramas of Hrotsvit of Gandersheim,* translated and with an intro-duction (Saskatoon: Peregrin Publishing Co., 1985), p. 7.

9. Peter Dronke, "Hrotsvit of Gandersheim," in his *Women Writers of the Middle Ages* (Cambridge: Cambridge University Press, 1984), p. 64.

10. Sandro Sticca, "Sacred Drama and Comic Realism in the Plays of Hrotswitha of Gandersheim," *Atti del 4 Colloquio della Société Internationale pour l'Etude du Théâtre Médiéval,* ed. M. Chiabò, F. Doglio, and M. Maymone (Viterbo: Union Printing Editrice, 1984), p. 151; see also Nagel, *Hrotsvit of Gandersheim,* p. 50; Helene Homeyer, *Hrotsvitha von Gandersheim* (Munich: Paderborn, 1973), pp. 44–45; Kurt Kronenberg, *Roswitha von Gandersheim* (Bad Gandersheim: C. F. Hertel, 1962), pp. 166–67.

11. Dronke, "Hrotswitha," p. 73; Katharina Wilson, "The Saxon Canoness: Hrotsvit of Gandersheim," in her edition of *Medieval Women Writers* (Athens: The University of Georgia Press, 1984), p. 36, writes: "Hrotsvit's reliance on hagiography in all her works is not man-ifested only in her choice of Christian saints and martyrs or exemplary virgins as her main characters. More fundamentally, it is reflected in her use of absolute moral opposites for the development of her themes." Ezio Franceschini, "Per una revisione del teatro di Rosvita," *Rivista Italiana del Dramma* 1 (1938), observes on p. 315 that "l'opera di Rosvita . . . è schietta-mente e squisitamente medievale, i suoi drammi non differiscono che per la forma dai poemetti agiografici suoi e dalle vite dei santi della tradizione" ("the work of Hrotswitha . . . is clearly and exquisitely medieval; her dramas differ only in their form from her hagiographical poems and from the lives of the saints of the tradition").

12. *Adversus Gnosticos Scorpiace, Patrologia Latina,* 2. col. 135. William C. Weinrich, *Spirit and Martyrdom* (Washington: University Press of America, 1981), remarks on p. 253 that "Tertullian came to regard Christian martyrdom as the very form and figure of the Christian life."

13. *In Evangelium Secundum Joannem, Patrologia Graeca,* 14. 1. col. 175: "qui ad mortem usque pro veritate et fortitudo decertarunt, conuetudo invaluit ut solos eos martyres appellarent."

14. On the subject see A. Rush, "Spiritual Martyrdom in St. Gregory the Great," *Theologi-cal Studies* 23 (1962): 569–89; also Gregorio Penco, "La spiritualità del martirio nel Medio Evo," *Vita Monastica* 85 (1966): 74–88.

15. *In Epistolam ad Hebreos:* 11, *Patrologia Graeca,* 63. col. 63. Anselme Stolz, *L'ascèse chrétienne* (Chevetogne: Edition des Bénédictins d'Amay, 1948), declares, p. 133, that "la vie ascétique, comme le martyre, exige en premier lieu la mortification" ("ascetic life, like martyr-dom, requires first of all mortification").

16. Louis Gougaud, *Ermites et Reclus* (Abbaye Saint-Martin de Ligugé, 1928), p. 31.

17. Louis Bouvier, *La spiritualité du Nouveau Testament et des Pères* (Paris: Aubier, 1966), pp. 379–80: "La solitude seule permet à l'homme de découvrir, et donc d'affronter, toutes les forces obscures qu'il porte en lui. . . . La solitude est une épreuve terrible car elle fait craquer et éclater le vernis de nos sécurités superficielles."

18. Etienne Delaruelle, "Les ermites et la spiritualité populaire," in *L'eremitismo in Occidente nei secoli XI e XII, Miscellanea del Centro di Studi Medievali,* vol. 4 (Milan: Vita e pensiero, 1965), p. 213.

19. Jean Leclercq, "L'érémitisme en Occident jusqu'a l'an mil," ibid., p. 44: "L'érémitisme est comme le martyre, une façon de pratiquer l'imitation de Jésus-Christ au maximum, parce que la solitude parfaite est ce qui exige le plus de renoncement et, finalement, malgré les apparences, d'amour."

20. Leópold Genicot, "L'érémitisme du 11e siècle dans son contexte économique et social," ibid., p. 49.

21. De Winterfeld, p. 162.

22. Kronenberg, *Roswitha von Gandersheim,* p. 195.

23. David Chamberlain, "Musical Learning and Dramatic Action in Hrotsvit's *Pafnutius,*" *Studies in Philology* 77 (1980): 319–43.

24. "Zu Hrotswithas Zeit die vier Lehrfächter des Quadriviums im letzten nur dazu dienten,

um den Mikrocosmos in Ubereinstimung mit den Makrokosmos zu bringen, dass heisst den Menschen zu Gott fuhren" (Homeyer, *Hrotsvitha von Gandersheim*, p. 240).

25. Leo Spitzer, *Classical and Christian Ideas of World Harmony* (Baltimore: Johns Hopkins Press, 1963), p. 55.

26. De Winterfeld, p. 167.

27. Ibid.

28. *St. Augustine. Of True Religion*, trans. J. H. S. Burleigh (Chicago: H. Requery Co., 1968), p. 34.

29. *Ad Epheseos* 2:19: "quia eratis illo tempore sine Christo, alienati."

30. De Winterfeld, p. 167.

31. Ibid., p. 168.

32. Ibid.

33. Ibid., p. 169.

34. Ibid., p. 179.

35. Ibid., p. 169.

36. Vernon J. Bourke, "Light of Love: Augustine on Moral Illumination," *Mediaevalia* 4 (1980): 12.

37. De Winterfeld, p. 171.

38. Ibid., p. 169.

39. Rabanus Maurus, in *Allegoriae, Patrologia Latina*, 112. col. 968.

40. *Alain de Lille. Textes Inédits*, ed. Marie-Thérèse d'Alverny (Paris: Librairie Philosophique J. Vrin, 1965), p. 271: "Ignis etiam luxuriae subtrahatur materia, ne mens concupiscat vana, ne sensus euagetur ad frivola."

41. De Winterfeld, p. 171: "Ne retineantur in mundo, quae male adquisivi, non absque mundi factoris iniuria."

42. Ibid., p. 173.

43. Ibid.

44. Ibid., p. 174.

45. Ibid.

46. Ibid.

47. Ibid., p. 175.

48. Ibid.

49. André Vauchez, *La spiritualité du moyen âge occidental. VIIIe–XIIe siècles* (Paris: Presses Universitaires de France, 1975), p. 59.

50. Herbert Grundmann, "Eremiti in Germania dal X al XII secolo: 'Einsiedler' e 'Klausner,'" in *L'eremitismo in Occidente nei secoli XI e XII*, pp. 311–329, 313.

51. De Winterfeld, p. 174.

52. Ann K. Warren, *Anchorites and Their Patrons in Medieval England* (Berkeley: University of California Press, 1985), p. 8.

53. "Solitaria sane vita coelestis doctrinae schola est, ac divinarum artium disciplina. . . . O cella negotiatorum coelestium apotheca . . . Felix commercium, ubi pro terrenis coelestia, in transitoriis commutantur aeterna. . . . O cella spiritualis exercitii mirabilis officina, in qua certe humane anima Creatoris sui in se restaurat imaginem, et ad suae redit originis puritatem! . . . O cella sacrae militiae tabernaculum . . . campus divini praelii, spiritualis arena certaminis, angelorum spectaculum, palaestra fortiter dimicantium luctatorum, ubi spiritus cum carne congreditur," *Laus eremiticae vitae*, in *Opusculum Undecimum. Ad Leonem Eremitam, Patrologia Latina*, 145. cols. 246–50, passim. Rabanus Maurus in his *Allegoriae, Patrologia Latina*, 112. col. 892, states: "Cella est Ecclesia, ut in Cantico: 'Introduxit me in cellaria sua,' id est, per contemplationem fecit me introire in gaudia interna" ("The cell is the Church, as in the Canticle: 'He introduced me in his storerooms,' that is, by means of contemplation he made me enter the internal joys").

54. Ibid., *PL*, 112, col. 247.

55. Ibid., *PL*, 112, col. 251.

56. *Liber numerorum qui in Sanctis Scripturis occurrunt, Patrologia Latina*, 83. col. 184.

57. *Sermones Centum, Patrologia Latina*, 177. col. 1109.

58. Ibid., col. 863.

59. De Winterfeld, p. 179. (Cf. *Psalm* 129:3: "Si iniquitates observaveris Domine, Domine quis sustinebit?").

60. De Winterfeld, p. 180. (Cf. Paul's *Ad Romanos* 11:6–7: "Si autem gratia, iam non est operibus: alioquin iam non est gratia" ("If out of grace, then is not by virtue of works: otherwise grace is no longer grace").

61. De Winterfeld, p. 180 (Cf. *Psalm* 148, passim, "Laudate eum coeli coelorum, et quae omnes, quae super coelos sunt . . . Montes, et omnes colles; arbores frugiferae, et omnes cedri . . . Ferae et omnia iumenta . . . Iuvenes et etiam virgines, senes, una cum pueris" ("Praise Him, you highest of heavens, and all you waters which are above the heavens . . . You mountains and all you hills; you fruit trees and all you cedars . . . you wild beasts and all you tame animals . . . You young men and you virgins, and you old men together with children").

62. *Patrologia Latina,* 83. cols. 189–94: "Hic autem [quindenarius numerus] mystice in duabus decisus partibus et praesens tempus significat, et aeternum demonstrat." And ". . . sicut in septenario numero presens vita volvitur, et designatur, ita per octonarium spes aeternae resurrectionis ostenditur." ("This moreover [the number fifteen] in its two mystical parts signifies present time and it indicates eternal time." And ". . . just like by the number seven it is designated the rolling of our present life, so too by the number eight the hope of eternal resurrection is demonstrated").

63. *Enarratio in Psalmum 6,* in *Patrologia Latina,* 36. cols. 90–91: "Potest quidem . . . dies judicii octavus intellegi, quod jam finem hujus saeculi accepta aeterna vita . . . Septenario numero transacto, quia unumquodque temporaliter agitur . . . veniet octavus judicii dies, qui meritis tribuens quod debetur, jam non ad opera temporalia, sed ad vitam aeternam sanctos transferet." ("The number eight can be understood to signify judgement day, in that with the end of this life eternal life is accepted. . . . Having gone through the number seven which is concerned with each temporal thing . . . comes the number eight signifying judgement day, when, having the due merits been allotted, the saints are brought over not to temporal works but to eternal life.")

64. *De numeris mysticis sacrae Scripturae,* in *Patrologia Latina,* 175. col. 22: "Octonarius ultra septenarius, aeternitatem post mutabilitatem." ("The number eight after the number seven signifies eternity after mutability.")

65. De Winterfeld, p. 180.

66. Ibid., p. 163.

67. Spitzer, *Classical and Christian Ideas of World Harmony,* p. 48.

68. De Winterfeld, p. 180.

Dante and the Virtues of Exile

GIUSEPPE MAZZOTTA

In his *Trattatello* Boccaccio devotes a substantial portion of the narrative to the description of the political turmoil that led to Dante's exile from Florence.[1] With an effort at impartiality that somewhat tempers the hyperboles of this essentially hagiographic text, Boccaccio does not shy away from remarking that Dante himself, with his stubborn arrogance, was not entirely free of responsibility in the tragic turn his personal life went on to take. After these statements, which perhaps because they are slightly unflattering have the appearance of factual truth, the flow of the narrative is interrupted. In a tone consistent with his stance throughout, Boccaccio proceeds to berate his public, the Florentine contemporaries to whom the text is addressed, for keeping Dante in exile even after their poet has long been dead and passionately urges them to retrieve his ashes from Ravenna.

The generous appeal clearly went unheeded, for Dante's ashes still lie away from his native city. Yet Boccaccio's failure to persuade the Florentines to perform an act of mercy and justice, which would have signalled the reconciliation of the city's divisions in the name of its poet, can in no way surprise us. If anything, one may be struck by a certain naivete in his belief that he could effect what Dante himself had failed to accomplish. At any rate, the fidelity with which Boccaccio paraphrases the exordium of *Paradiso* 25, where Dante utters the hope that he return to Florence to take the poetic hat, shows his conviction that the poet's genuine, if frustrated desire was to see the end of his exile.

The literalism in Boccaccio's understanding of Dante's voice is exemplary, for it prefigures countless subsequent efforts to bring the spirit of the poet "home." As is well known, these efforts range from the innocuous mock trials periodically held to establish Dante's guilt or innocence during the civil war of Florence to deliberate maneuvers to claim him as the founder of

This article originally appeared in *Poetics Today* 5, no. 3 (1984): 645–67. Permission to reprint it here is gratefully acknowledged.

latter-day political ideologies. It can doubtlessly be shown that these gestures to domesticate Dante, whether or not motivated by the benevolence of a kindred soul, inconsequential playfulness, or a dark calculus, are blind, for they sorely miss the point of Dante's radical insight into the nature of exile. Let me briefly illustrate this point.

In *Inferno* 15, the circle of the sodomites, Dante encounters his teacher Brunetto Latini. Brunetto asks his disciple by what fortune or chance he is journeying through the beyond and who it is that shows him the way. The pilgrim replies:

> "Là sù di sopra in la vita serena,
> rispuous' io lui, "mi smarrì in una valle,
> avante che l'età mia fosse piena.
> Pur ier mattina le volsi le spalle:
> questi m'apparve, tornand' io in quella,
> e reducemi a ca per questo calle."
>
> (49–54)

("Up above there in the bright life," I answered him, "before my age was at full, I lost my way in a valley. Only yesterday morning I turned by back on it. He appeared to me when I was returning to it and by this road he leads me home.")

Brunetto goes on uttering the prophecy of Dante's exile from Florence in terms that echo the pronouncements made earlier in the poem by Ciacco and Farinata. He also reassures him that if he follows his star, he will not fail to win a "glorioso porto."

The teacher's promise of success for his disciple's quest is a flagrant misunderstanding of all that is essential and unique in Dante's journey home, "a ca." The phrase, "glorioso porto," as the poet's destination that Brunetto predicts, is a way of drawing the pilgrim within the confines of the teacher's own experience, of assuming that his accessible goal, like Brunetto's, is the laurel of fame Humanists seek. But this is the canto where blindness has sway: Sodom is conventionally understood in patristic exegesis as "caecitas,"[2] and ironically the whole exchange between teacher and disciple measures the discrepancy between their respective visions, and shatters the impression of gentleness and dignity that lies at the surface of their encounter. Thus to Brunetto's prophecy of a contingent, historical exile to be later crowned by glory, Dante counters with an oblique correction:

> "Se fosse tutto pieno il mio dimando,"
> rispuos 'io lui, "voi non sareste ancora
> de l'umana natura posto in bando;
> chè'n la mente m'è fitta, e or m'accora,

la cara e buona imagine paterna
di voi quando nel mondo ad ora ad ora
m'insegnavate come l'uom s'etterna:
e quant' io l'abbia in grado, mentr'io vivo
convien che nella mia lingua si scerna.
Ciò che narrate di mio corso scrivo,
e serbolo a chiosar con altro testo
a donna che saprà, s' a lei arrivo.' "

(79–90)

("Were all my prayers fulfilled," I answered him, "you had not been banished from humanity; for in my memory is fixed, and now goes to my heart, the dear and kind paternal image of you when many a time in the world you taught me how man makes himself eternal; and how much I am grateful for it my tongue, while I live must needs declare. That which you tell of my course I write and keep with another text for comment by a lady who will know, if I reach her.")

The lines are quite clearly an acknowledgement of the values of humanistic education, but in the same breath the tribute recognizes the teacher's spiritual perspective as limited. For the aim of education, to teach man how he can make himself eternal, is at odds with the whole point of Dante's own journey. After all, the pilgrim's experience is meant to show that man can become eternal, can transcend the fragmentation of time ("ad ora ad ora"), not through the illusory project of man's own making, as Brunetto would want it, but through God's grace. The discrepancy between the two modes is lost on Brunetto, who oblivious of Dante's reminder that he is irrevocably exiled from humanity, still clings to the belief that he can go on living in the *Tresor,* the text he recommends to the pilgrim at the last farewell between them, as if to confirm his discipleship.[3] Against Brunetto's delusion, surely legitimate within a secular viewpoint, that the text is the locus where the self perpetuates its life, Dante evokes a view of writing, not as a self-enclosed and definite entity, but as an open commentary, an allegory, as it were, the sense of which will be disclosed by future glosses.[4]

If the teacher misunderstands, at least in part, the theology of exile that is the horizon of Dante's vision, it is small wonder that his disciple Boccaccio, as well as the humanists that follow him, did not seem to see much further. In truth, there is in Boccaccio's *Trattatello* something other than a banal encomium or literal-minded domestication of a Dante in pursuit of the laurel crown. Florence, Boccaccio argues, ought to be like the myriad cities of Greece that compete for the honor of being acknowledged as the birthplace of Homer.[5] Yet this is not the central concern of the story. Its brunt is that Dante's virtue goes unrecognized among his own people, and that even while living within the bounds of his city, he was engaged in a steady meditation on and experience of forms of exile. Dante is accorded the

highest merit, for instance, for bringing back the Muses to Florence from
their banishment; at the same time, the poet emerges from the legend as a
solitary man, who though not rootless and uncommitted in private and
public passions, keeps an essential distance from what surrounds him and
leaves behind "ogni . . . temporale sollecitudine" ("all temporal concerns"),
uncaring for, in words that overtly recall Dante's *Purgatorio* "fami . . . freddi
o vigilie" ("hunger, cold or vigils") in order to fathom the secrets of
philosophy and theology.[6]

What gives the account extraordinary power, however, is Boccaccio's
sense that Dante should be remembered solely by virtue of his being a poet.
The claim is such that Boccaccio is almost apologetic about shifting from
the pathos of the narrative to a digression on poetry's role in shaping man's
common awareness of the world. Deploying arguments that partly appear
in his *Genealogy of the Gentile Gods*,[7] Boccaccio dismisses the conventional
notion that poets are liars given to the cultivation of a hollow craft. By
evoking the mythic foundation of the world, he states that it was the task of
the poets to fashion it and inaugurate man's knowledge of it by their act of
naming. In effect, the poets are the first theologians, and the first name they
assign is that of "divinità," a generalized deity, while later they impart
names to the other gods. The belief in the theological origin of poetry leads
Boccaccio to assert that the nature of poetry is not significantly different
from the methods of representation employed in Scripture, which "quando
con figura d'alcuna istoria quando col senso d'alcuna visione quando con
l'intendimento d'alcuno lamento e in altre maniere assai mostranci l'alto
misterio dell'incarnazione del verbo divino" ("at times through the figure of
some story, at times through the sense of some vision, at times through the
understanding of some laments and in many other manners they show us
the high mistery of the incarnation of the divine word"). Theology, he
concludes with a statement that has the force of an aphorism, "niuna altra
cosa è che una poesia di Dio" ("is nothing else but God's poetry").[9]

This view of allegory as a common mode of significance for both poetry
and theology elides the sharp distinction that Dante himself draws between
the two in *Convivio* and the *Epistle to Cangrande,* where he explicitly claims
that the *Divine Comedy* is patterned on the paradigm of Exodus, the account
of the Jews' exile and return from Egypt to the Promised Land. The
relationship Boccaccio perceives between theology and poetry stops short
of Dante's insight about the link joining theology and poetry with exile.

I shall not be concerned here, then, with an inventory or articulation of
the theme of exile, which would be quite a legitimate topic of enquiry. Let
me simply say that it is well known that Dante has a thorough awareness of
himself as "exul immeritus" ("undeserved exile"), that in the *Divine Comedy*
there are specific references to all varieties of the experience of exile. Political
exile is countered by exile as a mode of man's being on earth, as an alien here
and a "peregrino" to Heaven.[10] Exile is a term designating the spiritual

condition of individual souls, as, for instance, in the line which tells of Boethius's or Cacciaguida's redemption, "e da esilio venne a questa pace" ("from exile he came to this peace").[11] One can also add that "eterno essilio" has the fixity of a formula to describe the state of the damned in Hell. But a theme, however accurate, tends always to be of questionable value because it arbitrarily restricts and isolates what by virtue of metaphor transgresses all bounds and cannot be hedged within boundaries of literal definitions. This is not an abstract *caveat,* to be sure, nor is it a veiled polemic against thematic criticism. It is, rather, Dante's own question about the way one can talk about exile, especially in the language of poetry, which philosophers and theologians had banished to the unreliable shadows of simulation or mere delightful ornamentation. To state it differently: Isidore of Seville under-stands exile, etymologically, as that which is outside.[12] A philosopher such as Boethius, and from this standpoint he marks the continuity of Plato in the Middle Ages, had dismissed poetry as meretricious and unfaithful because it offers itself to many.[13] At the same time Aquinas entertains a theological suspicion of the knowledge poetry yields.[14] But like Boethius, Aquinas is a poet, or to be more precise, he was a poet who abandoned poetry in favor of a rational univocal language that would lead fallen man along the path of the knowledge of God. Yet he never really ceased paying attention to the rift and complicity between theology and poetry—if one is to trust his remark, reported by his secretary Reginaldus of Piperno, that the theological work he had done could be easily interrupted, for "it was all straw."[15] Dante, the "theologus nullius dogmatis expers" ("theologian ex-pert in no dogma"), as we read in Boccaccio's *Trattatello,*[16] moves exactly within the problematic space where the discourse between poetry and theology is carried out and asks of theology and philosophy the very question he asks of poetry.

There is no doubt that in the *Divine Comedy* the writing of poetry is tied to the experience of exile. In *Paradiso* 17 the pilgrim asks his ancestor Cacciaguida to gloss for him the "parole gravi" ("serious words") he has heard about his own future. Cacciaguida replies at first by "chiare parole" ("clear words") with a prediction on the future course of the pilgrim's life and then exhorts him to deliver the truth of all he has seen.

> Tu lascerai ogni cosa diletta
> più caramente; e questo è quello strale
> che l'arco dello essilio pria saetta.
> Tu proverai sì come sa di sale
> lo pane altrui, e come è duro calle
> lo scender e 'l salir per l'altrui scale.

(55–60)

("You shall leave everything loved more dearly, and this is the shaft that the bow of exile shoots first. You shall prove how salt is the taste of another man's bread and how hard is the way down and up another man's stairs.")

Then Cacciaguida adds:

> "Coscienza fusca
> o della propria o del'altrui vergogna
> pur sentirà la tua parola brusca.
> Ma nondimen, rimossa ogni menzogna,
> tutta tua vision fa manifesta;
> e lascia pur grattar dov'è la rogna.
> Chè se la voce tua sarà molesta
> nel primo gusto, vital nodrimento
> lascerà poi, quando sarà digesta."

(124–132)

("Conscience dark with its own or another's shame will indeed feel your words to be harsh; but nonetheless put away every falsehood and make plain all your vision, and then let them scratch where is the itch. For if your voice is grievous at first taste, it will afterwards leave vital nourishment when it is digested.")

The poet's sense of his mission could hardly be overstated. Exile is the condition in which his voice rises, but the displacement does not entail a complacent isolation within a world largely indifferent to the private truth the poet witnesses. Actually the references to his own words as a palpable and edible substance place the poem within the tradition of the public utterances of biblical prophets.[17] Like the prophets, Dante makes of exile a virtue and a necessary perspective from which to speak to the world and from which he can challenge its expectations and assumptions; like the prophets, he also acknowledges that the truth he communicates is, paradoxically, what further alienates him from the world he has already lost.

The distance and confrontation between poet and world as the constitutive region of poetry is a persistent feature of Dante's moral imagination. Yet the poet's dwelling in a condition of exile contradicts on the face of it the statements repeated in a number of Dante's texts that his desire is to return to Florence. Such quite clearly is the case in the celebrated song of exile, "Tre donne intorno al cor mi son venute,"[18] to which I now turn.

The status of the poem in Dante's canon is made uncertain both by the additions that the poet is thought to have made later in his own life and by the reasonable belief scholars generally profess that Dante intended it as the last song to be commented in the fourteen books he had originally planned for *Convivio*. Since as is well known this treatise on ethics was interrupted with the fourth book, it is impossible to determine the sort of philosophical thinking Dante would have drawn from this poetic text. Taken by itself, the *canzone* is a transparent political-moral allegory of Justice.[19] As one of the virtues of the soul and the abstract subject of ethical speculation, Justice both affords and accounts for the double perspective of autobiography and allegory on which the movement of the poem hinges. The encounter between Self and the allegorical personification of Justice is staged at the outset of the first stanza with the three women who come to the poet's heart, where Love sits enthroned. One of them will identify herself later as "Drittura," but this is not Justice wielding the sceptre and other accoutrements of might, such as sword or crown. Actually, the vexed countenance of "Drittura" and her two attendant offspring (generally interpreted as natural and positive law) tell a story of sorrow: children of God and reigning once in the Garden of Eden, they are now despised outcasts who roam the world. By a powerful move, this exile of Justice is revealed in the poet's own personal exile:

> E io, che ascolto nel parlar divino
> consolarsi e dolersi
> così alti dispersi,
> l'essilio che m'è dato, onor mi tegno:
> chè, se giudizio o forza di destino
> vuol pur che il mondo versi
> i bianchi fior in persi,
> cader coi buoni è pur di lode degno.
>
> (73–80)

For all the proud distinction that the poet, made bold by the presence of the three lofty figures, sees in his exile, the reference to Justice's own consolation hints that the poet's claim may be another such attempt to be comforted, though consolation is not exactly what he seeks. The burden of the *canzone* is, in effect, an appeal that Mercy, the other daughter of God, may be shown to the poet, that the poem itself may generate desire for the flower of justice, as the first *congè,* picking up the metaphor of the white flower turned into a dark one, concludes: "e 'l fior, ch'è bel di fori/ fa disiar ne li amorosi cori" (99–100).

From this perspective, "Tre donne intorno al cor" brings to a head what has been anticipated in the first book of *Convivio:*

Since it pleases the citizens of the fairest and most famous daughter of Rome, Florence, to cast me forth from her most sweet bosom (where I was born and nourished up to the climax of my life, and wherein, by their good leave, I long with all my heart to rest my weary soul, and to end the days allotted to me) through almost every part where her language is spoken I have wandered, a pilgrim, almost a beggar displaying against my will the wounds of fortune.[20]

There is in the passage the prayer that the punishment of exile may be repealed. Yet the context also suggests that there may be a special value to the pilgrim's homelessness. In the preceding chapter, in fact, Dante records the admonition that to no man is it allowed to speak of oneself. The convention, Dante states, has been violated by Boethius and St. Augustine, who have deployed an autobiographical focus in *The Consolation of Philosophy* and the *Confessions,* respectively: in order for Boethius to remove the suspicion of infamy from his own exile, and in the case of St. Augustine, to set a useful example that others might emulate.[21] For Dante the immediate context for referring to his own personal experience of exile is to justify what could seem to be a lack of propriety and intellectual rigor in the philosophical commentaries he undertakes of his own poetry. But just as for Boethius consolation was a pretext to excuse "la perpetuale infamia de suo essilio, mostrando quello essere ingiusto, poi che altro escusatore non si levava,"[22] for Dante, too, philosophical thinking offers no consolation, but is itself at one with exile; or, more precisely, exile is the metaphor for his ongoing philosophical self-interrogation.

Even in "Tre donne intorno al cor" consolation has a provisional, but ultimately illusory and hollow value, which he must discard just as he discards other forms of self-deception. The references to the heart where Love dwells and reigns is in a way a conceit meant to imply the poet's moral integrity and lack of treachery; the three women come to the heart both to speak frankly of what is near to the heart's desire and because they "sanno ben che dentro è quel che dico" (18). Their guileless conversation, as if between friends, is in turn, a way of asserting the naked and open truth the poem will deliver to whatever friend of virtue it may find. There is, however, another doctrinal reason for the conceit: in reality, Dante raises the philosophical definition of Justice here. Consistent with the views commonplace since Plato, he understands Justice not as an intellectual virtue, the subject of and directed to speculative knowledge, but as a moral habit of the will, and the heart is the place of its dwelling. This doctrinal element governs other aspects of the poem.

In a way, since Justice is the internal ordering of man's will as well as the mark of social harmony, it is appropriately represented as a *dramatis persona* outside of the self, and the friend of Love residing in the heart. At the same time, since Justice is related to Good Venus ("Son suora a la tua madre," as she says to Love), the song appeals to the hearts in love to establish peace in the city. The poem's second *congè* begs precisely for the gift of peace:

> Canzone, uccella con le bianche penne;
> canzone, caccia con li neri veltri,
> che fuggir mi convenne,
> ma far mi poterian di pace dono.
> Però nol fan che non san quel che sono:

camera di perdon savio uom non serra,
chè 'l perdonare è bel vincer di guerra.

(101–107)

The stanza faintly echoes a passage from St. Augustine's *City of God:*

> Any man who has examined history and human nature will agree with
> me that there is no such a thing as a human heart that does not crave for
> joy and peace. One has only to think of men who are bent on war. What
> they want is to win, that is to say, their battles are but bridges to glory and
> peace. The whole point of victory is to bring opponents to their knees—
> this done, peace ensues. Peace, then, is the purpose of waging war.[23]

For St. Augustine the point is that "the peace of the irrational soul in the
harmonious repose of the appetites, domestic peace and civic peace"[24] all
prefigure the peace God promises in the Heavenly Jerusalem. But Dante
harbors no illusions, any more than St. Augustine ultimately does, about
the advent of peace. As we are told that "larghezza and temperanza," as well
as the other virtues themselves go begging (63–64), the song voices Dante's
tragic insight—fully deployed in the *Divine Comedy,* where the breakdown
of justice is so complete as to make this a satanic world—about the un-
feasibility of his heart's desire.

There are other elements in the poem that give weight to this darkening
of Dante's vision. The antithesis in the first stanza between "di fore," where
the three women coming round the poet's heart sit, and "dentro," (2–3)
where Love sits, suggests that for all their nearness there is still a distance
between these members of the same family. More importantly, as Justice
proclaims that the virtues, though wounded now, will live on, the statement
is at odds with Dante's presentiment of his own mortality, "che Morte al
petto m'ha posto la chiave" (87). This sense of death is the point in the poem
that marks the breakdown between the hope that the poet may return to his
city and the possible return of Justice. But Justice herself is involved in a
tragic predicament. As she begins her lament she is pictured resting her head
on her hand, "come succisa rosa" (21). The pathos that this image of
fragility and short-lived splendor conveys is intensified by its textual resonance. Derived as it is from the *Aeneid* (9.1.435), the allusion evokes the
deepest night of death in the whole of the Virgilian epic. It describes the
death of Euryalus, who having waited in vain to rescue his friend Nisus,
tumbles to the avenging fury of the Latins. The celebration of friendship
and the elegy for the two youths overwhelmed by the rage of war barely, if
at all, mitigate Vergil's representation of a relentlessly broken world, where
plunder and slaughter are the law and of which the Arcadian world of book
8 is the ironic setting. There is no doubt that this Virgilian echo is meant to
give a tragic perspective on Dante's allegory of Justice.

In the *De Vulgari Eloquentia* he refers to the three *magnalia*—*salus, virtus,* and *venus*—as the worthiest subjects to be treated by poets, and then he adds that the *cantio* is the most adequate form for the tragic style, appropriate to the treatment of those lofty themes.[25] In the *canzone,* "Tre donne attorno al cor," the voice is that of Melpomene, the Muse that wears the tragic mask: this is the tragedy of Justice, who, born in the Garden of Eden where she dwelled virginal, now roams corrupt and unrecognized through the world; who has reproduced herself in the guises of natural and positive law but goes disfigured and naked among men. Through the crisis of Justice, the poem also tells the tragedy of the poet himself, who acknowledges his estrangement from the world, who begs forgiveness but can only speak to hearts that only know strife. However, we are not to dismiss the call for a return from exile as a mere rhetorical gesture. The pathos of the poem comes precisely from the fact that there is a genuine desire for peace. The desire is accompanied by the poet's clear tragic knowledge of the futility of his efforts.

If in the first *envoi* of the song there is the implication of a truth available at the surface of the allegory (let no man touch the dress, let the uncovered parts suffice)—in the second *envoi,* the harder and darker truth emerges. Here there is an extraordinary deployment of rhetorical resources: the apostrophe to the *canzone,* metaphorized as a dove, the bird of Venus; an antithesis between "bianche" and "neri"; extended alliteration: Canzone, bian*che*, *cacc*ia, *u*ccella, *c*onvenne, pa*ce,* etc.; a *captatio benevolentiae;* a moral aphorism (107). The presence of these figures contrasts with the "parlar divino" (73), the unadorned language and appearance of Justice, as if the poet meant to dramatize his own best effort at rhetorical persuasion—the effort, that is, of inducing feelings of peace not harbored by his readers. At the core of the stanza, however, there is the acknowledgement that the gift of peace will not be made because his readers "non san quel che sono" (105). The line reverses the knowledge that at the end of the first stanza the three women are said to have ("ben sanno che dentro è quel ch'io dico"). The reversal seals the poet's awareness of the misunderstanding of his voice, as well as the failure of his rhetoric to persuade.

The perception of the tragic disintegration of Justice in the world of reality is carried over in the *Divine Comedy.* If the poem overtly enacts the unfolding of the "infallibile giustizia" as the "ministra/de l'alto Sire" (*Inferno* 29.55–56) in the system of punishments and rewards of the beyond; if it impatiently calls for the return of Astraea to the earth so that its original purity may be restored; if it privileges the epic of Roman history as nothing less than a providential instrument in the rule of law it deploys; and finally, if it singles out the justice and mercy of the Emperor Trajan, the poem also dramatizes the harsh lawlessness dominant in the actuality of political practice. "Lo mondo è ben così tutto diserto/d'ogni virtute come tu mi sone,/ e

di malizia gravido e coperto" ("The world is indeed as utterly deserted by
every virtue as you declare to me, and pregnant and overspread with
iniquity," Dante says to Marco Lombardo (*Purgatorio* 16.58–60), who goes
on to point out to the pilgrim the causes of the existing chaos. The blindness
of the world, Marco states, is due to the eclipse of the two lights of Rome,
and just as the light of the free will can relieve us of the burden and
deceptions of sin, so an emperor, who had at least some inkling of justice,
could at least discern the tower of the true city.

Since the moral crisis of the world seems to depend on a contingent crisis
of authority, it is possible to extrapolate a message of political optimism
from Marco Lombardo's speech. But Dante knows that fallen man is denied
the harmony of the Garden of Eden, and he also knows, as can be seen from
the encounter with Justinian, the emperor who codified the Roman law, that
the history of Rome can appear as a story of a lust for power and violence
against which the myth of its mission of universal justice crumbles. At stake
is the value of political history, punctuated, as it is in the *Divine Comedy,* by
the awareness of the persistent madness of civil war, an experience by which
every man is a stranger in his own home. The *Divine Comedy* is in a real
sense the tragic text of the civil war. From this perspective, Lucan's vision
and polemic with Virgil's ostensible celebration of the Empire become
Dante's own, not as a strategy to dismiss altogether the myth of political
order, but as signal of its unavoidable precariousness.[26]

In this formulation we are far removed from any simple notion of a
contrast between the order that the justice of the Empire embodies and the
provisional disorder of the times. The search for order in the community of
man is a steady concern for Dante at the very moment in which he
envisions, with a clarity that is hardly to be found anywhere outside of the
Divine Comedy, exile not just as a punishment inflicted by the power of a
man on another man, but as the truth of man's being in history. This
theology of exile is brought to focus quite appropriately in the examination
of the three theological virtues, faith, hope and charity, to which the pilgrim
is subjected respectively in *Paradiso* 24, 25 and 26.[27]

Critics who have discussed the cantos conventionally have stressed the
extent to which Dante's treatment of the three virtues moves within the
authorized canonical theological tradition. What is generally neglected,
however, is the conspicuous pattern in the cantos of both direct and oblique
references to exile—a pattern so clear as to indicate that exile, I submit, is the
textual horizon within which Dante is engaged in a powerful rethinking of
the theological virtues and, beyond that, in testing the nature of theological
language.

The opening lines of *Paradiso* 25 dramatize the pilgrim's exile from his
native city and express the hope that he may be allowed to return to Florence
and be granted the laurel crown. Later in the same canto, Beatrice antici-

pates the pilgrim's reply to St. James's question on hope by glossing Dante's journey to God in terms of the Biblical Exodus:

> "La chiesa militante alcun figliuolo
> non he con più speranza, com'è scritto
> nel sol che raggia tutto nostro stuolo:
> però li è conceduto che d'Egitto
> vegna in Ierusalemme, per vedere,
> anzi che 'l militar li sia prescritto."
>
> (52–57)

("The Church Militant has not a child more full of hope, as is written in the Sun that irradiates all our host; therefore it is granted him to come from Egypt to Jerusalem that he may see it before his warfare is accomplished.")

The lines overtly reveal the poet's exile and mission as the reenactment of Exodus, the epic of the return of the Jews from their captivity in Egypt to the peace of Jerusalem. The epithet "militante" for the Church echoes the pilgrim's "militare" and designates it not as the Church Triumphant, but as the Exodus Church, "in via," and makes of Exodus the paradigm of salvation history.

Paradiso 26 is almost equally divided between the examination on love by St. John and the pilgrim's exchange with Adam, who recounts his creation in the Garden of Eden, his fall, and redemption through Christ's Harrowing of Hell. The loss of the Garden is presented as an exile into an alien land: "Or, figliuol mio, non il gustar del legno/ fu per sè la cagion di tanto essilio,/ ma solamente il trapassar del segno" ("Now, my son, know that not the tasting of the tree in itself was the cause of so long an exile, but solely the trespass beyond the mark" [115–17]). Later Adam relates what could be called the diaspora of tongues, as he evokes the loss of the original unity and the construction of the Tower of Babel.

Paradiso 24, the canto of faith, itself bears only an oblique reference to exile, but it is framed by an explicit allusion to it. The final lines of canto 23 dramatize the pilgrim's astonishment and delight at the vision of the triumph of Mary and of the Church Triumphant:

> "Oh quanta è l'ubertà che si soffolce
> in quelle arche ricchissime che foro
> a seminar qua giù buone bobolce.
> Quivi si vive e gode del tesoro
> che s'acquistò piangendo nello essilio
> di Babilon, ove si lasciò l'oro."
>
> (130–33)

("Oh how great is the abundance that is stored in these so rich garners that were good sowers here below. Here they live and rejoice in the treasure they gained with tears in the exile of Babylon, where they spurned its gold.")

The thrust of the passage is the typological opposition, made familiar by St. Augustine's *City of God,* between the idolatry of gold at Babylon and the spiritual treasure of the Heavenly Jerusalem.[28] The word "ubertà," etymologically from *ubera,* the mother's udders, describes the generosity and fruitfulness of this place in terms of a garden of milk and honey, and as such is the central metaphor throughout the *Paradiso.* The opposition between Babylon and the Heavenly Jerusalem cannot be taken as absolute, for as the joy of Paradise comes forth as a recompense for the anguish suffered at Babylon, Dante casts exile as an ascetic and redemptive experience. More to our concern, within the typological context that immediately precedes it, the opening apostrophe of *Paradiso* 24, "O sodalizio eletto alla gran cena/ del benedetto Agnello, il qual vi ciba/ sì, che la vostra voglia è sempre piena" ("O fellowship elect to the great supper of the blessed Lamb, who feeds you so that your desire is ever satisfied" [1–3]), echoes the account of Exodus. For the convivial world of Heaven, which experiences God's bounty in its immediacy in fellowship, is the anagogical fulfillment of what appeared at the Last Supper in figure, the bread of affliction of Passover, which our fathers ate when they came out of the land of Egypt.

But the emphasis on the Paschal sacrament is of great moment because it provides a context in which we are brought up against the question of faith, the first of the three theological virtues. In contrast to the plenitude of the eschatological banquet, faith, like hope, is a virtue that belongs to the sphere of time. The emblem that describes the eternal dance of the souls as the revolving wheels in the structure of the clock (". . . come cerchi in tempra d'orioli si giran . . . *Par.* 24. 13–14), hints that we are bound to the domain of time as much as the pilgrim is. The metaphor of food eaten at this mystical banquet, moreover, gives a crucial twist to the understanding of faith. The canto is organized primarily as a confession of faith, as a statement of how faith reaches self-understanding. By combining tenets of Aristotelean-Thomistic philosophy with the Gospel teachings, the pilgrim confesses an essential faith both in one eternal God, who unmoved, moves all heaven with love, and in the unity and trinity of the godhead. Yet the object of faith is a faith in the event of the *kerygma,* the word of God recorded by the prophetic and apostolic texts. The definition of faith the pilgrim gives to St. Peter draws from and acknowledges the authority of St. Paul's epistle:

E seguitai: "Come 'l verace stilo
ne scrisse, padre, del tuo caro frate

> che mise teco Roma nel buon filo,
> fede è sustanza di cose sperate,
> ed argomento delle non parventi;
> e questa pare a me sua quidditate."

(Par. 24.61–66)

("As the truthful pen of your dear brother wrote of it, who with you, father, put Rome on the good path, faith is the substance of things hoped for and the evidence of things not seen; and this I take to be its quiddity.")

The pilgrim's faith, he goes on to say, comes to him from the plenteous rain of the Holy Spirit on the old and new parchments, and by believing the truth

> che quinci piove
> per Moisè, per profeti e per salmi,
> per l'Evangelio e per voi che scriveste
> poi che l'ardente Spirto vi fè almi;

(Par. 24. 135–38)

("which rains through Moses and the Prophets and the Psalms, through the Gospel and through you who wrote after the burning spirit made you holy;")

Retrospectively we can grasp the importance of the sacramental fullness that opens the canto. In a sense Dante would not accept the distinction between the Church of the Word and the Church of the Sacraments that arose from the theological debates that eventually would split European Christendom. Faith to him is faith in the tradition of the prophetic word, in its power to transform and contain reality and make the Revelation of the Word at one with history.

From one point of view, the acknowledgement of the authority of tradition frees the profession of faith from the domain of subjectivity and gives it a value that transcends the possibly arbitrary utterances of the individual self. Nonetheless, faith is exactly the virtue that cannot be separated from selfhood, and in St. Peter's summons to the pilgrim, "Di, buon cristiano, fatti manifesto:/ fede che è?" (52–43), the phrase "fatti manifesto" projects faith as a challenge to man to be seen and by the same token implies that faith reveals the very foundations of one's being.

What the Pauline definition of faith, which Dante quotes, reveals is first of all the temporality of one's life, for faith is the substance of hope, and thus places man in a world of time where he can only see through a glass darkly, beset by temptations and doubts. That faith is not the ground of absolute certainties is suggested in the canto by the brief speech in which Beatrice asks St. Peter to test ("tenta") the pilgrim "intorno della fede,/ per la qual tu su per lo mare andavi" ("regarding the faith by which you walked the sea" [*Par.* 24.37–39]). The allusion is to Matthew 14:29, where it is said that Peter walked on water to go to Jesus. Read in its entirety, however, the Gospel story tells of St. Peter, who while walking on the water, grows afraid of the wind and begins to sink but is caught by the hand of Jesus, who reproaches him, "O man of little faith, why did you doubt?" The scene is so crucial that Thomas Aquinas in the *Summa* employs it as the text to argue for degrees of faith, in which fear and doubt are never quite suppressed and which require the exercise of another virtue, that of courage.[29]

It is within the context of fortitude that we can understand why Dante always envisions the experience of faith in terms of an epic, with St. Dominic as the hero whose strength is tested in the daring warfare with the hydra of obstinate unbelief. Though without the legendary overtones that characterize the knightly adventures of St. Dominic, the pilgrim is also involved in a show of courage. Thus, he responds to St. Peter's test like a "baccellier" who arms himself for what amounts to an intellectual *certamen* with the Chief Centurion. This conjunction of metaphors drawn from the practice of university examination and the armed combat anticipates the formulation in *Paradiso* 25 of the Church Militant and the pilgrim's own "militar." More specifically, it depicts faith not just as a shield against error, but as a virtue that is inseparable from fear and intellectual risk.

The text sheds some light on the precise sense of this intellectual risk. There is, to begin with, an ironic counterpoint between the rhetoric and the statement on faith. The impression of the reasonableness of faith, conveyed by the series of questions and answers, is undermined by the fact that the content of faith is neither made up of analytical statements nor can be submitted to the rigor of philosophical investigation. Philosophy can provide proofs, which faith mobilizes to make its case, yet the extensive presence of the vocabulary of philosophy throughout the canto openly parodies philosophy's tacit assumption of reason's sovereignty. Thus, the rain the Holy Ghost poured over the Bible is a "syllogism" that establishes the truth in such a way that in comparison to it every demonstration is dull. More importantly, faith appears as the substance of things hoped for and the "argomento" of things not seen. The pains Dante takes in defining, first, "sustanza" as the ground that underlies and sustains hope, and second, "argomento" as the point of departure for reasoning (76–78), suggest his awareness of the complex theological reflections elicited by St. Paul's use of the term "argumentus."[30] At stake, I submit, is the nature of theological discourse, and, to put it most simply, the relationship between reason and faith.

Theologians such as William of Auxerre, Albert the Great and Thomas Aquinas agree that whereas in philosophy "argumentus" designates the rational process of persuasion with reason as the first principle, in theology its meaning is radically reversed. To the theologians "argumentus" describes the accountability of faith, the legitimacy in moving, when theological speculations are involved, from faith to those reasons that make faith credible. Fully conscious of the contradictory and double sense the word has in philosophy and theology, they explain the contradiction as a mark of the essential heterogeneity of the aims of the two disciplines.[31]

Dante subscribes to this rationale and in *Paradiso* 24 turns around the *modus argumentativus* of faith in order to expose the limits inherent in the sophist's wit ("ingegno di sofista" [81]). To him, and in this he follows the whole theological tradition, a faith that is fully rational has no merit. But Dante also gives a radical twist to St. Thomas's elaboration of the symbolic theology of the Pseudo-Dyonisius. Aquinas argues that there is no room for "argumentus," which belongs to scientific discourse, in the treatment of the metaphoric language of the Bible because metaphor by definition forbids the possibility of direct and precise knowledge. This insight is central to *Paradiso* 24, where, in effect, there is no proper definition of faith.[32]

St. Peter refers to faith obliquely as the "moneta," the alloy and weight of which have been examined, and then asks the pilgrim whether he has it in his purse. Dante replies: "Sì, ho, lucida e sì tonda,/ che nel suo conio nulla mi s'inforsa" ("Yes, I have indeed, so bright and so round that of its mintage I am in no doubt" [*Par.* 24. 86–87]). The etymological implication of "moneta," from "moneo," is a warning about the authenticity and preciousness of the imprint.[33] If one were to take the metaphor literally, however, there is an oddness to it, for money is a value that belongs to the kingdom of darkness, a worldly idol that counters St. Peter's and the poet's own indictment. From this point of view, it would appear that the tenor of the metaphor is to show how faith displaces and subverts what the world holds dear. More important, the coin, as a metaphor of exchange, makes faith, which is the bedrock of all other virtues, a metaphor with a power to redefine or dismiss the values of the world, but which itself lies beyond any proper definition. At the same time, if "argumentus" refers to a modality of theological speculation, "substantia" refers faith to another virtue, that of hope.

As in the discussion on faith, the examination by St. James on hope reveals the hope for the Resurrection of the dead and sees it as the general expectation of the fulfillment promised by the prophetic writings. The specific definition given, "attender certo / de la gloria futura" (*Par.* 25.67–68) discloses the nature of faith retrospectively; like faith, hope is a virtue of time, and, more precisely, it announces a belief in the future. In a sense, here lies the profound realism of hope, for it rejects as illusory the tendency to consider every experience as finite, or even to view the past as a closed and irretrievable experience. For the children of the promise, on the contrary, it is despair which is illusory; mistaking what is partial for the whole reality,

despair prematurely decides that everything is over and that the future itself
is empty. To have hope actually means that nothing is ever final, that the
future may have possibilities that may alter the contours of what in the
present one perceives as past and dead. If for the Greeks, who had no inkling
of this sense of hope, hope was a cheat, a self-willed blindness to the
unbearable pressures of life, for Dante hope is a form of desire that announces man's dislocation in the world of a future-oriented time, where a
necessary rupture exists between experience and the assessment of its value
and the present is the spot for man's waiting.

What a man of faith waits for, Dante says in *Paradiso* 26, is to live the
virtue of charity, the greatest gift of the Spirit and the foundation of all
Creation. After all, love, in the words of St. Paul, "bears all things, believes
all things, hopes all things, endures all things" (1 Cor. 13:4). In *Paradiso* 26,
however, there is not even an attempt to define the crown of the virtues,
both because the pilgrim's experience in the beyond, as well as the whole of
Paradiso, witness the reality of love and because love remains a persistent
mystery. The pilgrim has been blind throughout the examination on charity
conducted by St. John, the sharp-eyed eagle of love, and when Dante's sight
is restored as St. Paul's was by the virtue Ananias's hand he meets Adam,
who relates first his fall from the Garden into exile and later gives a brief
history of the languages of man.

It is possible to account for this shift from the virtue of charity to Adam's
original sin; the product of God's original act of love has been redeemed by
the loving sacrifice of the second Adam. More than that, this is the point
where we can grasp the profound reasons why exile systematically punctu-
ates this stretch of the text. In effect, the occurrence of the fall from the
Garden is not given merely as a theme, but is metaphorically rendered as an
exile into language. The prelapsarian tongue he used at Creation, Adam
states, was extinct before the building of the Tower of Babel. This explanation, as has often been remarked, substantially revises the theory Dante put
forth in his *De Vulgari Eloquentia,* where he writes that "a certain form of
speech was created by God along with the first soul. . . . In this form of
speech Adam spoke, and in this form also all his descendants spoke, until
the building of the tower of Babel, which is by interpretation the tower of
Confusion, and this form of speech was inherited by the sons of Heber,
who, after him are called Hebrews. The language remained with them long
after the Confusion, in order that our Redeemer (who was, as to His
humanity, to spring from them) might use not the language of confusion,
but of grace."[34] In the economy of the treatise the continuity of the language of grace allows Dante to envision grammar as the tool by which to
forge and order from the forest of multiple dialects one national language.

In *Paradiso* 26 there is a radical departure from this myth of a lingering
Edenic language. Forever subjected to the corruption of time, language is

the shifty ground of our knowledge; the Tower of Babel, Nimrod's unaccomplishable work, is the sign of the lonely foreignness of every voice. Grammar is still needed to halt the steady wearing out of words endangered by "uso" (137), which, though it is a norm for the agreement of sense, is like a leaf on a branch "che sen va e altra vene" ("That flies away and another comes" [138]). This instability involves the names of God, who was first called on earth "I" and later "El" (134–36). If in his discussion of the three theological virtues Dante clings to and deploys the truths of the theological language of the Bible, now, in the encounter with the original poet who has given a name to the Deity, he probes the nature of the language of theology.

The classical views on the question of the names of God are well known. For Dionysius, as he argues in *De divinis nominibus,* there can be no naming or opinion of God;[35] for Alain de Lille the names of God are ineffable because they signify the ineffable;[36] for Aquinas the word "God" is justified because it is used analogically.[37] "He who is"—the name that God applies to Himself in Exodus in response to Moses' question—is the most appropriate name for God because it implies a pure existence outside of any temporal sequence. "Even more appropriate," Aquinas writes, "is the *Tetragrammaton* which is used to signify the incommunicable and, if we can say such a thing, individual substance of God." Aquinas, realistically, is forced to straddle between agreeing with Dionysius that what we assert of God is loose "because no word used of him is appropriate to him in the way of signifying," and because "neither the Catholic nor the pagan understands the nature of God as he is in himself, and between the awareness that the words we use reflect the unavoidably composite way of understanding that our minds are capable of."[38]

In *Paradiso* 26 grammar, whose focus is the variations of time and words, can never reach God. In the changes that occur in the names that we use to call God, we confront the lack of any appropriate names available to us. If anything, the words we use for God reveal our yearning for and our distance from him. From this perspective poetry and theology, as Boccaccio had intuited, are linked together by the cloud of unknowing hovering over them. Radicalizing the insights of theologians such as St. Thomas, Dante invests poetry with what he calls a "divina virtù." In the protasis to *Paradiso* the poet begs to be filled, as if he were a passive vacant vessel, with Apollo's power and adds:

> O divina virtù, se mi ti presti
> tanto che l'ombra del beato regno
> segnata nel mio capo io manifesti,
> venir vedra' mi al tuo dilette legno,
> e coronarmi allor di quelle foglie
> che la matera e tu mi farai degno.

                                                    (1.22–27)

(O power divine, if you grant me so much of yourself that I may show forth the shadow of the blessed kingdom imprinted in my brain you shall see me come to your chosen tree and crown myself then with those leaves of which both you and the theme will make me worthy.)

So overt seems Dante's desire to receive the laurel in this invocation that it is small wonder that Boccaccio campaigned for his posthumous celebration. But we cannot be blind to the turn that these lines take in the unfolding of *Paradiso* 1, where the poet's rare triumph is presented in his embarking on a venture that will bring him and us in the nearness of God's presence, which is also the place farthest from him and where the holy is forever wrapped in mystery. Poetic language, and from Adam's speech we can infer all language, is the allegory of exile, the figure of man's displacement into an alien world.

Notes

All quotations from the *Divine Comedy* are taken from *La Divina Commedia secondo l'antica vulgata*, ed. Giorgio Petrocchi, 4 vols., Società Dantesca Italiana (Milan: 1966–67).

1. Giovanni Boccaccio, *Trattatello in laude di Dante,* a cura di Pier Giorgio Ricci (Milan, 1974).
2. Isidore of Seville, *Quaestiones in Vetus Testamentum,* in *Patrologia Latina* (henceforth cited as *PL*) 83. col. 246 A–B; Gregory, *Moralia in Job,* in *PL* 750. col. 750 B; more generally, cf. the definition, "Sodoma interpretatur caecitas," in *PL* 113. col. 131 B.
3. *Inferno* 15.119–20. For an extended discussion of the whole passage see the pages devoted to it in my *Dante, Poet of the Desert: History and Allegory in the Divine Comedy* (Princeton, 1979), pp. 138–41.
4. "Ciò che narrate di mio corso scrivo,/ e serbolo a chiosar con altro testo/ a donna che saprà, s'a lei arrivo." *Inferno* 15.88–90.
5. *Trattatello,* p. 461.
6. *Trattatello,* p. 443. Cf. *Purgatorio* 29. 37–38.
7. For the passages in the *Genealogy of the Gentile Gods,* see *Boccaccio, on Poetry,* ed. Charles G. Osgood, The Library of Liberal Arts (New York, 1956), pp. 35–39.
8. *Trattatello,* p. 472.
9. *Trattatello,* p. 475.
10. "O frate mio, ciascuna è cittadina/ d'una vera città; ma tu vuo' dire/ che vivesse in Italia peregrina" ("O my brother, each one here is a citizen of a true city: but you mean one that lived in Italy while a pilgrim" [*The Divine Comedy of Dante Aligheri,* trans. Charles S. Singleton, 3 vols. Princeton University Press, 1975]). All translations of the *Divine Comedy* are taken, unless otherwise indicated, from Singleton's text. (*Purgatorio* 13.94–96).
11. The line refers to Boethius, *Paradiso* 10.129. Cf. also "e venni dal martirio a questa pace" ("and I came from martyrdom to this peace") (*Paradiso* 15.148). For the typological resonance of the line, see *Dante, Poet of the Desert,* p. 126.
12. "Exilium dictum quasi extra solum. Nam exul dicitur qui extra solum est." 5.27, 28 in *Etymologiarum sive originum Libri 20,* ed. W. M. Lindsay (Oxford, 1966).
13. *De Consolatione Philosophiae,* trans. H. F Stewart, Loeb Classical Library (Cambridge, Mass., 1958), 1, prose 1.
14. "Poetry employs metaphors for the sake of representation, in which we are born to take delight. Holy teaching, on the other hand, adopts them for their indispensable usefulness, as just explained." *Summa Theologiae* 1. q. 1. art. 9, resp. The English text is from the Blackfriars edition (New York, 1964).

15. For the full account of this radical change of mind, see Josef Pieper, *The Silence of St. Thomas,* trans. John Murray (New York, 1957), pp. 89 ff.

16. *Trattatello,* p. 459.

17. "Thy words were found, and I ate them; and Thy words became a joy to me, and the rejoicing of my heart" Jeremiah 15:16. See also the similies in *Isaiah* 55:10–11.

18. The text that follows is taken from Dante's *Rime,* a cura di Gianfranco Contini (Turin, 1964), pp. 174–79. The translation is taken from Kenelm Foster and Patrick Boyde, *Dante's Lyric Poetry,* 2 vols. (Oxford, 1967), 1:174–81. Permission to reprint this material has been granted by Giulio Einaudi Editore and by Oxford University Press.

Tre donne intorno al cor mi son venute,
e seggonsi di fore;
ché dentro siede Amore,
lo quale è in segnoria de la mia vita.
    Tanto son belle e di tanta vertute,   5
che 'l possente segnore,
dico quel ch'è nel core,
a pena del parlar di lor s'aita.
    Ciascuna par dolente e sbigottita,
come persona discacciata e stanca,   10
cui tutta gente manca
e cui vertute né beltà non vale.
Tempo fu già nel quale,
secondo il lor parlar, furon dilette;
or sono a tutti in ira ed in non cale.   15
Queste così solette
venute son come a casa d'amico;
ché sanno ben che dentro è quel ch'io dico.

    Dolesi l'una con parole molto,
e 'n su la man si posa   20
come succisa rosa:
il nudo braccio, di dolor colonna,
    sente l'oraggio che cade dal volto;
l'altra man tiene ascosa
la faccia lagrimosa: 25
discinta e scalza, e sol di sé par donna.
    Come Amor prima per la rotta gonna
la vide in parte che il tacere è bello,
egli, pietoso e fello,
di lei e del dolor fece dimanda.   30
'Oh di pochi vivanda',
rispose in voce con sospiri mista,
'nostra natura qui a te ci manda:
io, che son la più trista,
son suora a la tua madre, e son Drittura;   35
povera, vedi, a panni ed a cintura.'

    Poi che fatta si fu palese e conta,
doglia e vergogna prese
lo mio segnore, e chiese
chi fosser l'altre due ch'eran con lei.   40
    E questa, ch'era sì di pianger pronta,
tosto che lui intese,
più nel dolor s'accese,
dicendo: 'A te non duol de gli occhi miei?'
    Poi cominciò: 'Sì come saper dei,   45
di fonte nasce il Nilo picciol fiume
quivi dove 'l gran lume
toglie a la terra del vinco la fronda:
sovra la vergin onda

generai io costei che m'è da lato   50
e che s'asciuga con la treccia bionda.
Questo mio bel portato,
mirando sé ne la chiara fontana,
generò questa che m'è più lontana.'
    Fenno i sospiri Amore un poco tardo;   55
e poi con gli occhi molli,
che prima furon folli,
salutò le germane sconsolate.
    E poi che prese l'uno e l'altro dardo,
disse: 'Drizzate i colli: 60
ecco l'armi ch'io volli;
per non usar, vedete, son turbate.
    Larghezza e Temperanza e l'altre nate
del nostro sangue mendicando vanno.
Però, se questo è danno,   65
piangano gli occhi e dolgasi la bocca
de li uomini a cui tocca,
che sono a' raggi di cotal ciel giunti;
non noi, che semo de l'etterna rocca:
ché, se noi siamo or punti,   70
noi pur saremo, e pur tornerà gente
che questo dardo farà star lucente.'

    E io, che ascolto nel parlar divino
consolarsi e dolersi
così alti dispersi,   75
l'essilio ch m'è dato, onor mi tegno:
    ché, se giudizio o forza di destino
vuol pur che il mondo versi
i bianchi fiori in persi,
cader co'buoni è pur di lode degno.   80
    E se non che de gli occhi miei 'l bel segno
per lontananza m'è tolto dal viso,
che m'have in foco miso,
lieve mi conterei ciò che m'è grave.
Ma questo foco m'have   85
già consumato sì l'ossa e la polpa
che Morte al petto m'ha posto la chiave.
Onde, s'io ebbi colpa,
più lune ha volto il sol poi che fu spenta,
se colpa muore perché l'uom si penta.   90

    Canzone, a' panni tuoi non ponga uom mano,
per veder quel che bella donna chiude:
bastin le parti nude;
lo dolce pome a tutta gente niega,
per cui ciascun man piega.   95
Ma s'elli avvien che tu alcun mai truovi
amico di virtù, ed e' ti priega,
fatti di color novi,
poi li ti mostra; e 'l fior, ch'è bel di fori,
fa' disïar ne li amorosi cori.   100

    Canzone, uccella con le bianche penne;
canzone, caccia con li neri veltri,
che fuggir mi convenne,
ma far mi poterian di pace dono.
Però nol fan che non san quel che sono: 105
camera di perdon savio uom non serra,
ché 'l perdonare è bel vincer di guerra.

1. Three women have come round my heart, and sit outside it, for within sits Love who holds sway over my life. They are so beautiful and of such dignity that the mighty Lord, I mean him in my heart, almost shrinks from speech with them. They each seem sorrowful and dismayed, like those driven from home and weary, abandoned by all, their virtue and beauty being of no avail. There was a time, to judge from their account, when they were loved: now all regard them with hostility or indifference. All alone, then, they have come as to the house of a friend, for they know well that he of whom I speak is here.

2. One of them begins to lament bitterly, resting her head on her hand like a clipped rose: her bare arm, a column for grief, feels the rain that falls from her eyes; her other hand conceals the tear-stained face: ungirt and barefoot, only in her person does she reveal herself a lady. When Love first saw, through the torn dress, that part of her which it is decent not to name, in pity and anger he asked about her and her grief. 'O food of the few', she replied, her voice mingled with sighs, 'it is our kinship that makes us come to you; I, who am the saddest, am sister to your mother; I am Justice—poor, as you see, in dress and girdle.'

3. When she had revealed herself and made herself known, sorrow and shame seized my lord, and he asked who were the other two with her. And she, who had wept so readily, no sooner heard him than she kindled with yet more grief and said: 'Have you no pity on my eyes?' Then she began: 'As you surely know, the Nile springs, as a little stream, from its source there where the great light takes the osier-leaf from the earth: by the virgin wave I brought forth her who is at my side and who dries her tears with her yellow hair. She, my fair child, gazing at herself in the clear spring, brought forth her who is further from me.'

4. His sighs made Love falter a little: then, with eyes moist that before had been heedless, he greeted his unhappy kinsfolk. And then, seizing both his arrows, he said: 'Lift up your heads: here are the weapons I have chosen—weapons, you see, that are tarnished from disuse. Generosity and Temperance and the others born of our blood go begging: and yet, though this is a disaster, let the eyes that weep and the mouths that wail be those of mankind whom it concerns, having fallen under the rays of such a heaven; not ours, who are of the eternal citadel. For though we are wounded now, we shall yet live on, and a people will return that will keep this arrow bright.'

5. And I who listen to such noble exiles taking comfort and telling their grief in divine speech, I count as an honour the exile imposed on me; for if judgement or force of destiny does indeed desire that the world turn the white flowers into dark, it is still praiseworthy to fall with the good. And were it not that the fair goal of my eyes is removed by distance from my sight—and this has set me on fire—I would count as light that which weighs on me. But that fire has already so consumed my bones and flesh that Death has put his key to my breast. Even if I was to blame for it, the sun has now circled for several moons since that was cancelled, if blame dies through repentance.

Congedo (1). Song, let no man touch your dress to see what a fair woman hides; let the uncovered parts suffice; deny to all the sweet fruit for which all stretch out their hands. But should it ever happen that you find someone who's a friend of virtue, and he should ask you, put on fresh colours and then show yourself to him; and make the flower that has outward beauty be desired by hearts in love.

Congedo (2). Song, go hawking with the white wings; song, go hunting with the black hounds—which I have had to flee, though they could still make me the gift of peace. It is because they don't know what I am that they don't do so: a wise man will not lock the chamber of forgiveness; for to forgive is fine victory in war.

19. For a bibliography and the canonical understanding of the poem see the entry by Mario Pazzaglia in the *Enciclopedia dantesca* (Rome, 1976), vol. 5, pp. 709–11.

20. *Il Convivio*, ed. G. Busnelli and G. Vandelli, rev. A. E. Quaglio (Florence, 1964), 1:iii, 4–5. The English text is taken from *The Banquet*, trans. Katharine Hillard (London, 1889), pp. 11–12.

21. *Convivio*, 1:ii, 12–15.

22. *Convivio*, 1:ii, 13–14. The passage in its entirety reads: "And this necessity it was that moved Boethius to speak of himself, in order that, under the pretext of consolation, he might defend himself against the perpetual infamy of his exile, showing how unjust it was, and since no other apologist came forward." *The Banquet*, trans. K. Hillard, p. 9.

23. St. Augustine, *The City of God,* trans. Marcus Dods (New York: 1950), 19.12, p. 687.

24. *The City of God* 19.13, p. 690.

25. *De Vulgari Eloquentia,* ed. Aristide Marigo, rev. Pier Giorgio Ricci (Florence, 1968) 2:2.8–9. For the tragic style of the song, see 2.6.6.

26. See for an extended exploration of the issue my *Dante, Poet of the Desert,* especially pp. 3–65.

27. The traditional readings of the three cantos are best exemplified by the views put forth by Adolfo Jenni, N. Rodolico and E. Donadoni, respectively, on *Paradiso* 24, 25, and 26 in *Letture Dantesche. Paradiso,* ed. G. Getto (Florence, 1961), pp. 483–548.

28. *The City of God* 16.4 and 20. 17 for Babylon and Jerusalem, respectively.

29. *Summa Theologiae* 2a 2ae, q. 5, art. 4, as opposed to *S. T.* 2a 2ae, q. 7. Aquinas discusses whether "timor" is an effect of faith.

30. Hebrews 11:1.

31. The range of the debate is carefully examined by M. D. Chenu, *La Théologie comme science au 13ᵉ siècle* (Paris, 1969), pp. 32–52 and 58–68, especially.

32. "Fede è sustanza di cose sperate/ e argomento delle non parventi;/ e questa pare a me sua quiditate" ("Faith is the substance of things not seen; and this I take to be its quiddity") (*Paradiso* 24.64–66). Faith is clearly defined in terms of another theological virtue, hope. Later in the canto faith is referred to in terms of the metaphor of a "coin." That the "proper" definition of faith is doubtless a theological problem of some moment is made evident by St. Thomas's remarks in the *Summa Theologiae,* 2a 2ae, q. 4, art. 1.

33. "Moneta appellata est quia monet ne qua fraus in metallo vel in pondere fiat." Isidore of Seville, *Etym.* 16.16.8.

34. *De Vulgari Eloquentia* 1.6.4. The English text is taken from *De Vulgari Eloquentia,* trans. A. G. Ferrers Howell (London, 1973), pp. 23–24.

35. For the importance of the text see *Summa Theologiae,* 1. q. 13, art. 1, obj.

36. See Reg. 21 in Alanus de Insulis, *Regulae De Sacra Theologia,* PL 210. col. 631. For a survey of the problem in terms of its grammatical and theological implications, see M. D. Chenu, "Grammaire et théologie aux 12ᵉ et 13ᵉ siècles," *Archives d'histoire doctrinale et littéraire du Moyen Age,* vols. 10 and 11 (1935–36): 5–28.

37. *Summa Theologiae,* 1, q. 13, art. 10, resp.

38. *Summa Theologiae,* 1, q. 13, art. 11, resp.; and art. 12, resp.

Unamuno in Exile

RANDOLPH D. POPE

Born in 1864, don Miguel de Unamuno was fifty-nine years old when he read that Primo de Rivera's government had decided to deport him to Fuerteventura, a desolate region in the Canary Islands.[1] According to a local journalist, Unamuno read the edict in a newspaper, while strolling in Salamanca's Plaza Mayor. He continued his walk as if nothing had happened, always the teacher or the actor. On the following day, 21 February 1924, he left the city, where he had been president of the university from 1900 until deposed for political reasons in 1914 and where he had continued teaching Greek, distinguishing himself more as a novelist, philosopher, and journalist than as a scholar. He was widely respected, always called *don* Miguel, although he was controversial and an activist who plunged happily into any situation where speech could be an irritant to thought. He condemned king Alfonso XIII's tendency toward German militarism and did not hold back his criticism after the disastrous African campaign. When general Primo de Rivera came to power in 1923 with a proclamation that identified his new strong Directory with manly virtues, Unamuno scoffed and wrote to a friend in Argentina a derisive letter against the Spanish government. This letter found its way into a Buenos Aires magazine and provided one of the reasons for don Miguel's exile. He then gave a talk in Bilbao that was considered, probably justly, inflammatory. Curiously, later on he will insist that the edict did not give any reasons for his exile. He must have known what they were, or at least have clearly suspected them, but he was setting a trap, hoping that the government would indulge in a debate with him concerning the legitimate reasons of exile. They knew better. In Salamanca he was near the geographical center of Spain, but his removal to the last frontier of Canarias strengthened his voice.[2] After three months on the island, where he wrote political and mystical poems celebrating the sea, he escaped in a ship provided by his French publisher. By the end of his stay in Fuerteventura Unamuno had received a pardon that he refused to accept, since it would have implicitly acknowledged his guilt. During a year spent in Paris he wrote, in two spurts of activity separated by several months, the first part of *Cómo se hace una novela, How a Novel Is Made.* It was translated into French by his close friend Jean Cassou and published in the *Mercure de France* in 1926. By the end of August of 1925, Unamuno had moved to Hendaya, a French Basque town close to the border of Spain. Here, two and a half years later, Unamuno will decide to retranslate into Spanish *Cómo se hace una novela* from Cassou's French version, while inserting some additions to the previous text and making some final entries in the form of a continuation and a diary. In spite of a growing interest in *How a Novel Is Made,* many questions remain unanswered, among them most crucial of all: how does this text express the experience of exile. The main character is don Miguel himself; therefore I wish to underline that the text should be approached with the same care required by any autobiography. Critics who have taken the statements of the textual don Miguel to be those of don Miguel himself or, as he would have said, the dead one, the one who was killed and survived by the written one, have been misled into accepting every statement as sincere or rejecting it as hypocritical. I observe a writer at work writing about his image of a writer at work. This will prove to be a crucial distinction. The centrality of exile is expressed forcefully:

> For I had conceived the idea, some months ago, of writing a novel in which I would put down the most private experience of my exile and thereby create myself, eternalize myself under the signs of banishment and proscription. And now I consider that the best way to make this novel is to tell how it should be made. This is the novel of a novel, a creation of a creation. (p. 734)[3]

Why did he decide that the best way to write a novel conveying the deepest expression of his exile was merely to tell how it should be written?[4] Did these instructions that failed to bring forth the real product, a full-fledged novel, express the language of the exile condemned to linger in cafés abroad and to imagine what may happen, but incapable of having any effect in the mainstream of national history? This interpretation is sustained by the narrator's insistence on his idle and painful frustration: "How awful to live in expectation, wondering each day what tomorrow may bring! And what it may not bring! I spend hours at a time, alone, stretched out on the bed of my small hotel, or 'family house,' contemplating the ceiling of my room instead of the open sky and dreaming of the future of Spain and of my own future. Or: unraveling it. And I do not dare to begin any sort of work, because I cannot be sure of being able to finish it in peace" (729–30). The idea is repeated later in the text: "But the worst of it is that I was not writing anything of importance. I had sunk into a state of painful, anticipatory inactivity, thinking about what I would do or say or write if this, that, or the other thing happened, dreaming the future, which is the same (as I have said before), as to unravel it" (736). Like Penelope, the exile awaits the return of the hero, only deceivingly (but not to himself) active, stringing words together, or undoing an invented future, "deshaciéndolo." What has been called by one critic monstrous and unfinished and has been considered by others a mere metanovelistic exercise or even a clever anticipation of Derridean thought[5] is for me the metaphor itself of the experience of exile, as Unamuno clearly stated it, his most private (and, therefore, universal) experience of exile, "la más íntima experiencia de mi destierro." The place of exile is a place where projects do not find their way into practice, where they whirl in the mind and on the page as shaky substitutes for action. Almost fifty years later, another self-exile, Juan Goytisolo, also wrote a novel about the thoughts of a character who could be a writer named Juan Goytisolo, and who daydreams in Africa of the invasion and destruction of Spain. In this novel of 1970, *La reivindicación del conde don Julián,* in which the unnamed character can see Spain from the seashore as Unamuno could from Hendaya, Goytisolo will stress the cyclical nature and ineffectiveness of this dream. Unamuno, after interrupting his project for a few months, had found the best structure to make his predicament evident. A finished novel would have given the illusion of accomplishment, precisely what he wished to short-circuit because it would have made his exile look creative. Indeed, Ferrater Mora looks back at Unamuno's exile as an example for him of the good old days, and many critics assess this period as positive in Unamuno's development as a writer.[6] It may have been so, since after his return in 1930 he would write some of his major works. But the instructions to write a novel stand as the open wound of exile, a wound that rejects any literary balm and can only be sutured by returning to the homeland. Unamuno, if anything, stressed the miserable conditions of life abroad in order to embarrass the Spanish government. Quite possibly the fact that he left behind his wife and children, who only came to see him for brief vacations, was intended not only to spare them the pains of exile, but also to increase his own suffering and play his role to the hilt: "Eternalize myself under the signs of banishment and proscription" ("eternizarme bajo los rasgos de desterrado y de proscrito").

    He had found a role model in Mazzini, the Italian patriot who spent most of his life in exile while laboring for the ultimately successful unification of Italy. With characteristic repression of any aspect that could diminish his own originality, (he will employ a similar maneuver in relation to Nietzsche)[7] don Miguel mentions in *Cómo se hace una novela* Mazzini's letters as if he had read them just by chance. He had, in fact, quoted Mazzini before, shown an interest in his work, and felt deeply in harmony with his political ideas and practice.[8] He must have snatched away the book of Mazzini's letters to Judit Sidoli offered to him by an Italian exile, Alcestes de Ambris, those letters of "aquel otro proscrito que fue José Mazzini," and one assumes that the other is don Miguel himself. Both share another aspect besides their exile, and that is love for a distant woman. Don Miguel approvingly quotes Mazzini's letter to Judit Sidoli in which he wrote that it was impossible for him to write a novel about his experience because then he would have to make public his love for her. Since Judit's father-in-law was a powerful enemy of Mazzini and had kept custody of her chidlren, this had to be avoided. Don Miguel declares that he also has written about his love for his wife in his sonnets, with the conclusion being that he could not write a novel that would not become autobiographical. Unamuno speaks only of "her Judit" ("su Judit" [731, 747]), leading at least one critic to believe that Judit was Mazzini's wife.[9] In fact, she was the widow of another Italian exile. She probably had a child from Mazzini, but she abandoned her lover when she grew cooler to his grand illusions of revolution and freedom. Mazzini glossed over the episode by coming to believe that he himself had sent her away to her children and safety, in order to better devote himself to his mission.[10] Unamuno believed off and on that he had been chosen by God himself to become a priest, and that as a consequence of turning down this invitation and marrying his childhood love, Conchita, he had been punished with an incapacity to feel a sincere faith. This paradoxical predicament would find an outlet with the order of exile, which with one stroke liberated him from his family and university obligations, what he called his Salamanca cage. Once, when one of his sons read a particularly somber poem don Miguel had written in Paris and became alarmed, he warned Conchita, who decided to follow don Miguel to France. Apparently Unamuno wrote a brusque letter to his daughter that hurt his wife by implying that if she joined him she would just be in his way.[11] Thus, while Mazzini is used by Unamuno to stress his love for Conchita, it seems possible that don Miguel patterned much of his valued suffering solitude after Mazzini's lonely wanderings through Switzerland and England, and a wife with three or more children following her would not have cut the proper figure. Perhaps too, Regina Olsen's fate in the life of the mission-driven Kierkegaard, another of Unamuno's alter egos, reinforced this profile of heroic loneliness. He feared becoming a tourist and understood the acute solitude of exile as a discipline to keep the soul alert and uncompromising.

Also difficult to unravel is the question of the confessed motivation for writing *How a Novel Is Made*. "Under these circumstances and in such a state of mind, some months ago, after I finished reading Balzac's terrifying *Peau de chagrin,* the plot of which I knew and which I devoured with growing anguish, here, in Paris and in exile, it occurred to me to put myself into a novel that would be a kind of autobiography" (731). Clear similarities in argument have already been pointed out by other critics: Valentin in Balzac's novel is a young scholar out of money and luck who receives the gift of a wild ass's skin.[12] This skin will allow Valentin to get everything he wishes, but it shrinks with each wish granted, showing how life is thereby shortened. U. Jugo de la Raza, Unamuno's character's character, lives alone in Paris and reads a fascinating novel that contains a sentence condemning the reader to die at the end of the book. Valentin's entourage of friends and lovers has been completely excised in Unamuno's version of the story. This Faust, the origin of both Valentin and U. Jugo de la Raza, does not even have a servant or disciples. Since, as I have proven above, deep solitude is peculiar to exile as seen by Unamuno, it was natural that the bohemian friends, the faithful servant, and the loving admirer would disappear.

Less evident is why Unamuno considered Balzac's novel a motivation to write about his own exile. It has been suggested that the book Jugo buys near the frozen river Seine represents history, and reading it Jugo is disenchanted with his comfortable, uneventful life and drawn by the harsh and dangerous lure of political action.[13] As Valentin desires something to happen and his life is thereby shortened, so Jugo—according to this theory—by participating in the theater of history, by becoming a character of the collective novel of social life, loses his own true self and hastens his death. Also, it is well known that Unamuno had had cardiac problems and had been obsessed by death. Jugo plays macabre games with himself, believing that as soon as he reaches the next tree he will fall dead (p. 738). It is possible that Unamuno believed that when he finished this project of a novel he would die, and thus he postponed and prolonged it. But how does all of this relate directly to exile? And there is a flaw with the neat theory described above. Jugo, in the 1925 version, manages to avoid finishing reading the book and even burns it. Ultimately he travels and finds another copy but apparently resists the temptation to finish it. The novelist does not provide us with an ending. At that time, 1925, don Miguel was fully acting out his political persona, and it seems contradictory that he would keep his character from dying if that was what was needed to participate in the stream of history. In the 1927 additions Jugo is saved from reading by returning to the region of his childhood, much as don Miguel did when he went to live in Hendaya, not abandoning for a moment his political struggle. This was even more embarrassing to the Spanish government, as it constituted a living scandal right at the border. They tried several times in fact to have him removed by the French authorities, a failure that don Miguel narrates with relish. It has not been sufficiently stressed that Jugo is a reader absorbed by the character of the novel, since his own life lacks reality, much as don Miguel's seems to have ebbed away at the tertulias in Paris and Hendaya. It has not been noted that Jugo is bored because "now, he doesn't live except in himself, in that poor ego passed over by history" ("no vive ya más que en sí mismo, en el pobre yo de bajo la historia" (734) meaning with this all-important *ya* that at some other time—before exile—he did live in history. True existence seems to be elsewhere, the past or the novel, and the character does not resist his curiosity. It is in this reading, not by acting in history but following it, that the self is diminished. The exile is absorbed by the news, never really new, mediated writings, most of the time disparate and of the past, and he comes to depend on the life at home, failing to develop a true independent existence. Valentin tries to repress his desires, Jugo his curiosity, since desire and curiosity empty them of their own selves. This interpretation is supported by a series of sentences clearly overlooked by other critics in the hope of providing a transcendental interpretation of Jugo's problems:

> Meanwhile [Jugo] asked himself: "How will this story end?"
>
> And I asked myself something similar when I imagined that passage in my novel: "How will the story of the Directory end, and what will the fate be of the Spanish monarchy and of Spain?" And I devoured—as I will continue to devour—the newspapers, and awaited letters from Spain. (741)

Can a better description be given of the situation of the exile, who hates or despises the government who has exiled him, but nevertheless pines for news and is constantly occupying his mind with Primo de Rivera, Castro, or Pinochet? The sucking away of his own existence is so complete that when they, the dictators, die his own life is without direction, as was Juan Goytisolo's, one of Franco's most vehement enemies, when he was or-phaned by the dictator.[14] Jugo manages to resist this abjection by coming back to a place, to nature and infancy, where history falls into perspective as a transitory activity enveloped by eternity. Valentin in Balzac's novel also tries to recover in the country, but it is a countryside of hotels and servants where he is followed by brutal civilization and forced to desire the death of an opponent in a duel. But for Unamuno there is a greater countryside, where only nature speaks in eternal presence and silence. Here new strength can be found to act in history without losing oneself in someone else's story.

Two problems remain to be explored. Unamuno asserts that he had given the original manuscript to Jean Cassou and that he would translate it from the French because he did not wish to recover the original text, "no quiero recobrar el texto original" (710). This is startling. Apparently he associated those pages with so much suffering that he did not wish to see them again: "I am not at all sure how I would react to the sight of those prophetic pages that I wrote in that little room of my great solitude in Paris" (710). The mediation of French allows him to remove the aura of the original and see it more as a reproducible text. Translation becomes a distancing activity, interposing Cassou between Unamuno-1925 and Unamuno-1927. In fact, Cassou is treated badly, even if we are told elsewhere that he was Un-amuno's best friend in Paris and that he called him "Juan." For the *Mercure de France* Cassou had written a rather attractive portrait of Unamuno, that don

Miguel proceeds to translate in 1927. He then comments upon Cassou's portrait, tearing it apart. I am more interested in the event itself than in the details of his disagreements with Cassou, mostly well-thought out and ingenious modulations of Cassou's observations; don Miguel first translates the portrait and then scribbles his own refinements and contradictions over it. He could simply have left it out altogether, but he is like someone showing off a photograph in which he is truly dreadful. There is the pleasure of correcting paper with flesh and blood, the imprint of the past with the immediacy of the present. Given the sense of unreality brought about by exile, this affirmation of existence is especially pleasurable. More-over, exile, in most cases, is the fate of a misunderstood being, since most exiles believe that they have been wronged, as Unamuno certainly did. The fact that Cassou, who knew him well and was his "querido Cassou," did not understand him thoroughly, is only one more instance of these mispercep-tions that don Miguel could not let go unchallenged.

In Balzac's novel there is a peculiar case of translation that don Miguel must have found amusing. The wild ass's skin bears an inscription in Arabic, but the antiquarian and Valentin seem to believe it is Sanskrit. As it is doubtful that Balzac is translating the Arabic text (it was translated for him from French to Arabic by the orientalist Baron von Hammer-Purgstall) and then incorrectly identifying the language it is written in, it is also improba-ble that Unamuno was truly translating from Cassou's French version, especially when he had been so critical of the portrait. Is this just another case of Unamuno's vanity, of his showing off his knowledge of French, as he loved to insist on his readings of Kierkegaard in the original? Or were the memories awakened by the manuscript so painful that he truly preferred not to face them? At the very least, this gesture increases the desolate portrayal of the exile that he wished to present. But it also introduces a wedge between 1927 and 1925, the point at which the original manuscript was lost. This loss is chosen and sustained, as I will explain later, for a deeper motive.

The second problem is the additions of 1927. As readers, we are ac-customed to second and revised editions. As is the case with most products of our economy, work is hidden by presenting a surface where sentences from the first and second edition look alike. Only critical editions reawaken the variants and recover the process of thought and intervening labor. Unamuno did not choose the path of icing over his disparities with that (deliberately) unrecoverable original text. He added twenty comments re-garding his 1925 version, and he did so by presenting them bracketed. He painstakingly explains at the end of his comments to Cassou's portrait:

And now I move on, to retranslate my narration of how a novel is made. And since it is impossible for me to replace it without rethinking it, that is to say without reliving it, I will be forced to comment it. And as I would like to respect as far as possible the person I was, the one who lived through that winter of 1924 to 1925 in Paris, whenever I add a commentary I will place it within square brackets, thus: [ ]. (727)

This seemingly childish insistence emphasizes the importance of this unique method of signals, markers that clearly, unmistakably, separate the Unamuno who was in Paris from the one he was in Hendaya. He will not be assimilated into one coherent figure for comfortable classification. It is symptomatic that Zubizarreta, who studied the book in great detail, passes blindly over these bracketed additions, attempting to prove that there is nothing new in them and that don Miguel remains consistent.[15] Why do so many critics worry about Unamuno's consistency, when the writer himself did not? For example, Ilie in the introduction to his excellent book explains: "Since Unamuno could not change his personality even if he wanted to, he continued to make digressions and parenthetical remarks throughout his essays. The result was an ostensibly inconsistent philosophy. However, an internal analysis of these textual divergences reveals a completely coherent and often unvaried statement on a given question."[16] But, to Unamuno's probable amused agreement, Ilie goes on to write a few pages later: "His writings are . . . contradictory and, indeed, irreconcilable in the final analysis" (p. 46). Inés Azar presents all three versions of *Cómo se hace una novela* as united in an organic body, and thereby saved from time.[17] I believe, on the contrary, that it is precisely the different selves in different times that Unamuno wishes to record, introducing all possible wedges—translation being one—to keep the past and present selves separate. His opinions at times are clearly contradictory. Without smoothing over his change he shoots down from within the brackets the opinions he had in 1925. In one case, for example, he had spoken about a repentant Primo de Rivera and about Unamuno's love for members of the Directorio (p. 745). He can see in 1927 that he had been led astray in 1925 by his depressive mood and probably by the fascination of expressing paradoxical ideas, his love hidden by hate, and the fictional character of Primo and Anido. The inscription of this contradiction between 1925 and 1927 is probably what his writing is all about. He had already written in 1914: "To renew oneself or to die, it is said. It applies, of course, to thought as well as to a person. Thought that does not renew itself, dies. Or, what is the same, it becomes commonplace. And the renewal of thought is rectification."[18] He does not wish to be arrested in a sentence, to die in a book, as a character in the history of literature. What the text shows in its breaks and starts, its interruptions and contradictions, is the living imprint of a man moving in time. When Primo de Rivera called Unamuno "incorrigible" he was exactly wrong.[19] Unamuno was determined to show him in exile that he could correct himself, that he would not be reduced to a phantom reader of newspapers and letters, that he would continue to grow and change, that he could not be detained. So he adds to the previous text of *Cómo se hace una novela,* already shot through with brackets, translated, a "Continuación", begun 4 June 1927, and finished on 17 June, ending with the apparently definitive line, "And so it is, reader, how a novel is done and finished for ever" ("Y así es, lector, cómo se hace para siempre una novela" [762]). And so it is that he keeps on going right after this previous ending, for seven more days, from 21 June to 7 July, resting only after the seventh day of renewed, incessant creation.[20] Clearly he has proven his point: in exile the worst danger is stagnation and loss of self, the worst pains, loneliness, ineffectiveness, and dread. The answer to these dangers and sufferings can be found in the continued transformation of the self, the rescuing of a time corroded by repetition by underscoring the freedom of the mind and resisting the oblivion of the old, courageous, selves that burned to ashes in Fuerteventura, Paris, and Hendaya leaving behind their irreducible light of words. How does one read *Cómo se hace una novela?* Certainly, taking into account Unamuno's expressed will, it must be read as a description of the experience of exile.

Notes

1. For Unamuno's biography, see Emilio Salcedo, *Vida de don Miguel* (Salamanca: Anaya, 1964).

2. Sebastián de la Nuez offers a detailed account of don Miguel's exile in the Canary Islands, *Unamuno en Canarias. Las islas, el mar y el destierro* (Canarias: Universidad de la Laguna, 1964).

3. I translate from the 1966 edition of the *Obras completas,* vol. 6 (Madrid: Escelicer), pp. 707–69. For a history of the creation of the text and of its editions, consult Armando F. Zubizarreta, *Unamuno en su nivola* (Madrid: Taurus, 1960), and Allen Lacy, "Censorship and *Cómo se hace una novela,*" *Hispanic Review* 34 (1966): 317–25. There is an English translation by Anthony Kerrigan, published in *Novela/Nivola* (Princeton: Princeton University Press, 1976), pp. 381–481.

4. I agree on this point with the opinion of Inés Azar, "La estructura novelesca de *Cómo se hace una novela,*" *Modern Language Notes* 85 (1970): 184–206, who does not interpret the "ahora" to mean that he abandoned the previous plan, but rather that he had modified it.

5. Julián Marías calls *Cómo se hace una novela* "a brilliant but not fully realized book" (p. 59 of *Miguel de Unamuno* [Cambridge: Harvard University Press, 1966]). David G. Turner speaks of "the rambling and disjointed diary of a man suffering the agonies of exile" (p. 107 of *Unamuno's Web of Fatality* [London: Tamesis, 1974]). Paul Olsen offers a brilliant Derridean reading in "Unamuno's Lacquered Boxes: *Cómo se hace una novela* and the Ontology of Writing," *Revista Hispánica Moderna* 36 (1970–71): 186–199.

6. José Ferrater Mora, *Unamuno: Bosquejo de una filosofía* (Buenos Aires: Losada, 1944), pp. 34–35. Ricardo Gullón, in *Autobiografías de Unamuno* (Madrid: Gredos, 1964), writes: "Alfonso XIII y Primo de Rivera le ayudaron, persiguiéndole y confinándole, a escribir su novela personal" (p. 261). Luis S. Granjel, in *Retrato de Unamuno* (Madrid: Guadarrama, 1957), even believes that "Unamuno aceptó, y me atrevo a decir que complacido, el papel de proscrito" (p. 313).

7. For a consideration of the Nietzsche/Unamuno dialogue, consult Paul Ilie, *Unamuno: An Existential View of Self and Society* (Madison: University of Wisconsin Press, 1967), pp. 123–126.

8. Vicente González Martín, in *La cultura italiana de Miguel de Unamuno* (Salamanca: Universidad de Salamanca, 1978), pp. 150–58, describes Unamuno's knowledge of Mazzini's

work and concludes that don Miguel must have read the Italian exile for the first time around 1908. Cf. also Gaetano Foresta, "Miguel de Unamuno: comentario sobre Mazzini," *Cuadernos de la Cátedra Unamuno* 21 (1971): 5–17.

9. Zubizarreta, twice, pp. 76 and 343.

10. Mazzini writes in a letter to Luigi Amedeo Melegari, dated London, 8 April 1937: "For a long time she has sacrificed me to duty and to her children—as was right, and as I myself begged her to do" (*Mazzini's Letters* [Westport: Hyperion Press, 1930], p. 41). For this episode, see the stark study by Stringfellow Barr, *Mazzini, Portrait of an Exile* (New York: Holt and Co., 1935), where we find this pleading letter to his lover: "Your letters, each syllable, a silence, an erasure—I have studied them all, and some of them—why should I not tell you?—inoculated me with death" (p. 99).

11. Zubizarreta, pp. 267–68.

12. Cf. Gullón, pp. 274 and 284; also the brief article by Martin Nozick, "Unamuno and *La peau de chagrin*," *Modern Language Notes* 65 (1950): 255–56.

13. Frances Wyers, in *Miguel de Unamuno: The Contrary Self* (London: Tamesis, 1976), writes: "*Cómo se hace una novela* shows the failure of every attempt to solve the dilemma of inner self vs. legendary self" (p.55).

14. Cf. my interview with Juan Goytisolo in *Espejo de escritores,* ed. by Reina Roffé (Hanover, N.H.: Ediciones del Norte, 1985), p. 118.

15. Zubizarreta, pp. 106 y 107.

16. Ilie, p. viii.

17. Azar, p. 201.

18. "Arabesco pedagógico sobre el juego," *Obras completas,* vol. 8, p. 309.

19. Primo de Rivera in "El Presidente del Directorio contesta a la carta abierta de *El Liberal*," *El Liberal* (Madrid), 4 November 1924, p. 1, calls Unamuno "notoriamente incorregible." On the reaction of the Government to Unamuno's activities as an exile, see Víctor Ouimette, "El destierro de Unamuno y el ataque a la inteligencia," *Cuadernos de la Cátedra Unamuno* 27–28 (1983): 25–41.

20. Unamuno would have found a kindred spirit in Foucault, as can be seen by the latter's introduction to *The Archaeology of Knowledge:* "I am no doubt not the only one who writes in order to have no face. Do not ask who I am and do not ask me to remain the same: leave it to our bureaucrats and our police to see that our papers are in order. At least spare us their morality when we write" ([New York: Harper, 1976], p. 17). (*L'Archéologie du Savoir* was first published in Paris by Gallimard in 1969.)

The Muse of Exile:
Estrangement and Renewal in Modern Irish Literature

GEORGE O'BRIEN

1

In order for Stephen Dedalus "to forge in the smithy of my soul the uncreated conscience of my race," three preconditions were necessary, as he asserted in a celebrated phrase: "silence, exile and cunning" (*P,* 247). Of the three terms, "exile" is by far the most telling, the one most likely to evoke imaginative sympathy. And its significance is reinforced by the fact that it is a condition common both to Stephen's aspirations and Joyce's strategy for voicing them.

Author and subject are not identical, however. Joyce was a committed exile (inasmuch as he remained abroad), but psychically he never left Dublin. Early and late in his career he was critical of Ireland, but he tempered the bitterness of estrangement from Dublin by desiring "for a few persons of character and culture to make Dublin a capital such as Christiania has become."[2]

On the other hand, Stephen in *Ulysses* is a failed exile, and not only on geographical grounds. We accept that he had to return from Paris—although perhaps a decision to remain there would not have been as great an affront to his dying mother as his behavior at her bedside. The source of his failure is artistic. The conscience of Stephen's race is as inchoate in *Ulysses* as ever it was. But this present ability to perceive "the soul of that hemiplegia or paralysis which many consider a city" (*SL,* 22) more accurately and to describe it to himself less rhetorically and more cynically hardly seems to help. The need for artistic renewal—more disciplined, more intense, more heretical than Buck Mullingan's flippant, Wilde-derived Hellenism—is at least as urgent as before. But, "Welcome, O life!" (*P,* 252) are not the words of the man portrayed as a young artist in *Ulysses.*

There is, however, a characteristic common to the protoexile of Stephen

Dedalus and the actual exile of his maker. In both cases there is a movement outwards—an expression of expansiveness and of self-assertion—which has as one of its foremost implications a realignment with what has been forsaken. Closer intimacy with the native realm, a more graphic, unsparing and comprehensive revelation of home, improvements in perspective, focus and vision: these are the fruits of absence. And since exile is voluntary, may it not be that such rewards are being deliberately sought? At any rate, Stephen's willingness to depart and take up apprenticeship in the artistic-spiritual "smithy" serves the hope of cultural renewal, even flippantly: "The shortest road to Tara is *via* Holyhead" (*P*, 250). And there is Joyce himself, writing from exile in connection with *Dubliners:* "My intention was to write a chapter of the moral history of my country . . ." (SL, 83).

"Ireland was Joyce's fate, a condition of his being with which he could come to terms only through rebellion."[3]

A movement—essentially of the mind, but in Joyce's case of sufficient psychic urgency as to require a geographical counterpart—which proceeds from absence to realization, from estrangement to intimacy, may also be discerned in Yeats's working out of his relationship to Ireland. Whether the poet is berating "this unmannerly town"[4] or noting, on Paudeen's behalf, that "there cannot be, confusion of our sound forgot / A single soul that lacks a sweet crystalline cry" (*CP*, 122); whether he is dreaming of fairyland, codifying the phases of the moon or resenting "the seeming needs of my fool-driven land" (*CP*, 109), there is a characteristic action of Yeats's mind that places it in a disposition of withdrawal or remoteness in order that it attain more penetrating vision. Again, as in Joyce's case (indeed, in a phrase reminiscent of Stephen Dedalus's overture to the smithy), the objective is "to write for my own race" (*CP*, 166).

The movement of withdrawal does not, for Yeats, require the same geographical specificity as it did for Joyce. The action's range has a more exclusively literary provenance, as suggested by the poet's efforts to renew a love of "old Eire and the ancient ways" (*CP*, 35) by means of Mallarmé's poetics. (The cultural expression of the verse's essay in harmony is also conceived of in terms of range and reconciliation: "the sole test . . . / Dream of the noble and the beggar-man" [*CP*, 369]). Yet even in the matter of geography, Yeats's habit of locating himself in places sympathetic to his artistic and cultural program is more deliberate than Joyce's. Sligo is an antidote to London. Thoor Ballylee keeps at bay, as best it can, the crushing pressure of the historical moment. And there was the poet's Lough Key project. On "an island all castle . . . I planned a mystical Order." Yeats's account goes on:

> for ten years to come my most impassioned thought was a vain attempt to find philosophy and to create ritual for that Order. I had an unshakea-ble conviction arising how or whence I cannot tell, that invisible gates

would open as they opened for Blake, as they opened for Swedenborg, as they opened for Boehme, and that this philosophy would find its manuals of devotion in all imaginative literature, and set before Irishmen for special manual an Irish literature which, though made by many minds, would seem the work of a single mind, and turn our places or beauty of legendary association into holy symbols.[5]

For Joyce, there was the metropolis in protean syzygy; for Yeats, the metropolis and its other. For both, to "turn aside and brood" (*CP,* 49—the phrase haunts Stephen in *Ulysses* and typifies his mood) is a habit of mind that outlasts the desire to be relieved of it.

"Yeats can never find escape in his dreams, for they all lead more or less circuitously back to action."[6]

The consciousness of the Irish artist, as embodied jointly by Yeats and Joyce, is estranged from the reality that is its subject. Indeed, if that reality— the constituent elements of which are cultural, political, racial, historical, and religious—is to be apprehended artistically, a condition of withdrawal, displacement, and alienation must be undergone. Yet the outcome of this artistic *rite de passage* is not to enter a world larger than the Irish one, but to make the Irish world large enough to enter. The reconstruction of Irish reality using foreign-made tools of consciousness renders estrangement redemptive.

Renewal as an entailment of departure is not perhaps an entirely Irish phenomenon. Eliot, concluding *Four Quartets,* comes to mind:

> We shall not cease from exploration
> And the end of all our exploring
> Will be to arrive where we started
> And know the place for the first time.

And of course Joyce and Yeats are spokesmen for the restlessness of modernism, as well as architects of its containment. Yet, unlike many of their fellow-modernists, national origins and native place continue to have a leavening effect and a mediating role throughout the oeuvres of Yeats and Joyce. Ireland endures as subject and object of imaginative commitment, sometimes as pretext and sometimes as target, but always presumed to be amendable to aesthetic reconditioning. Such fidelity may not be attributed to Conrad, Pound, Eliot himself, Lawrence (though he hoped it could), Nabokov . . .

Irish writers following the example of Yeats's and Joyce's dedication to art, however, articulate their commitment in terms that obey the founding fathers' pattern of withdrawal and revelation, intimacy and alienation, absence and return, rejection and renewal. The persistence of that Joyce/Yeats "movement" is the subject of what follows.

Geographical exile is not required in order that the pattern manifest itself fully. Two of the writers to be discussed below, the novelist Francis Stuart (b. 1902) and the poet Dennis Devlin (1908–59), were strongly influenced by their international experiences. The other two writers, however, the novelist Flann O'Brien (1911–66) and the poet Thomas Kinsella (b. 1928), are exiles who never in any significant sense left home. Despite the enormous variations of tone, intellect and ambition delimited by this quartet, all are united—quite possibly, against their will—in the history of a posture. They are all the more brothers-in-art by virtue of the formal strategies and accidents of temperament that individuate them. And, by any reckoning, they are the most significant bearers of the artistic tradition in Irish letters, Yeats and Joyce inaugurated.

To raise the question of a tradition of whatever kind in an Irish context is to open floodgates of imprecision and complexity. Irish history, culture, and literature are friable compounds of competing and often antithetical interests and emphases. Such compounds make for cultural richness, but they do not lend themselves readily to reproduction in stable intellectual models. Nevertheless, for the present purpose the following generalizations may be risked.

Irish writing from the mid-1920s onward adopted two main orientations, neither of which was on good terms with the other. A sociocultural orientation expressed itself most significantly in prose and verse satire. It also meditated on the recent Irish wars in tones and forms (short fiction, particularly) derived from the nineteenth-century masters, notably Turgenev. The main exponents of the resulting lyrical naturalism (although it is probably more accurate to see the results as an expressionism skeptical of nerve and sinew) are Frank O'Connor and Sean O'Faolain. The most worthwhile achievements in the sociocultural realm of prewar Irish letters, however, are the revisionist romances and satires in prose and verse of Austin Clarke, which, apart from their verve and daring, provided a point of aesthetic departure for O'Brien and Kinsella.

In contrast, an artistic-spiritual school of Irish writing went to Proust and Dostoievsky for its prose models and for verse found stimulus in Valéry, Claudel and Eluard. Beginning in the 1930s, Francis Stuart and Denis Devlin broadened already-existing emphases on self rather than on society, on spirit instead of matter, on love rather than on time, as does the work of their great contemporary, Samuel Beckett. By rejecting the plausibility of what *Finnegans Wake* calls "a commodius vicus of recirculation" in any context whatsoever (except perhaps the aesthetic and formal, where it enacts an ironic ritual of cohesion), Beckett's work helps to focus the significance of Stuart's ardent pursuit of renewal and Devlin's embattled hope of it. Understandably, neither writer found it possible to espouse such nullifying evenhandedness as,

It is suicide to be abroad. But what is it to be at home, Mr. Tyler, what is it to be at home? A lingering dissolution.[7]

On the contrary, the challenge accepted by Stuart and Devlin was to outwit such a state of affairs.

2

The appearance of the short-lived periodical *To-morrow*, in 1924, is a convenient point from which to date the commitment of Joyce's and Yeats's heirs. The periodical's first editorial promised a provocative stance and a visionary program. Written by Yeats, it concludes

> No man can create, as did Shakespeare, Homer, Sophocles, who does not believe, with all his blood and nerve, that man's soul is immortal, for the evidence lies plain to all men that where that belief has declined, men have turned from creation to photography. We condemn, though not without sympathy, those who would escape from banal mechanism through technical investigation and experiment. We proclaim that these bring no escape, for new form comes from the human soul restored to all its courage, to all its audacity. We dismiss all demagogues and call back the soul to its ancient sovereignty, and declare that it can do whatever it please, being made, as antiquity affirmed, from the imperishable substance of the stars.[8]

This statement's lofty rhetoric and its emphasis on removal and renewal reveal the new artistic dispensation's severe integrity. In cultural terms, however, the editorial anticipates—or perhaps intimates—a state of tension between the writer and his world, a condition codified by that triumph of what George Orwell, in another context, called "smelly little orthodoxies": the Censorship of Publications Act of 1929. This piece of legislation confirmed all Irish writers as Shelleyan "unacknowledged legislators," speaking, in Yeats's phrase, "the language of the outlaw,"[9] and constituting, by virtue of their heterodoxy, a government in exile. As a recent historian of the period has observed:

> But the fact remains that Irish repressiveness, whatever its cause, was extreme in those first crucial decades after independence, and that it severely stunted the cultural and social development of a country which a protracted colonial mismanagement had left in desperate need of revival in both spheres.[10]

Among the signatories of the *To-morrow* editorial was a young poet, Francis Stuart. Born in Australia in 1902, Stuart was reared in Ulster, attended English public schools (notably Rugby), and at eighteen married Iseult Gonne. In Yeats's lines, "a girl who knew all Dante once / Lived to bear children to a dunce" (*CP,* 388), Stuart is the last-mentioned. Yet along with other less important figures of the thirties, Yeats was, in Stuart's own words, "extraordinarily generous to me."[11]

If Yeats numbered himself among "the last romantics," Stuart may be described as the ultimate romantic. Such a designation derives from the integrity and consistency with which he held his original artistic ground. In *Things to Live For* (1936), he declares: "I will remain with those on . . . the frontiers. With the gamblers, wanderers, fighters, geniuses, martyrs and mystics . . . the storm-troops of life."[12] And in a 1975 interview, he continues to describe himself as "a writer of dissent. . . . I believe that loneliness and pain are necessary for certain writers whose best work comes from not being absorbed into even a very sympathetic milieu."[13] Although he realized that "the romantic, the inspiring, the lyrical, will always be a lost cause in this dark age which is organized for businessmen and commerce" (*TTLF*, 42–43), nevertheless he persisted "in search of that romance that cannot be counterfeited, that is stark and cold and harsh like the smell of water and the noise of leaves" (*TTLF*, 16), stimulated, evidently, by the thought that "the end of all romance must not be the gaining of anything, not possessing, but sacrifice" (*TTLF*, 58). Not surprisingly, the spate of novels produced by Stuart in the thirties after his early flirtation with verse (twelve novels in all between 1931 and 1939) have as their theme spiritual craving.

The most important of these—*Pigeon Irish, The Coloured Dome,* and *Try the Sky*—all locate a concern for the soul of Ireland in a hypersensitive female protagonist, who is prepared to suffer, even unto death, rather than compromise her longing for purity, renewal, and hope. Outsiders, men at a loss culturally and spiritually (and who sometimes drift in aimless continental exile), are drawn to these protagonists, with whom they find their morale restored and the future worthwhile.

These novels offer, but do not realize, the prospect of social accomplishment. Real attainment is shown to be intimate, private, inward. Composure of personality and tenacity of purpose will, it seems, have an inevitably beneficial influence on and elevate the principles of contemporary Irish life. The narrative mode is projective, not recapitulatory; the outlook is more visionary than critical; Stuart's disposition is improvisatory, morally heterodox and intensely forward-looking.

In the futuristic *Pigeon Irish,* there is a fear that Ireland will succumb to "a civilisation that has been refined to rottenness."[14] The narrator, Frank Allen, comes to accept the credo of his anima, Catherine Arrigho, which is: "We can only save Ireland from being engulfed, by suffering. Like the early Christians. . . . They kept the faith by being martyred" (*PI,* 79). Frank and Catherine's means of rendezvousing with destiny (or uniting "at the holy place of execution," *PI,* 276) is to be more extreme in their cultural demands than the status quo can admit. Their revolutionary commitment places them beyond the pale of duly-constituted authority. They run a gauntlet of psychic travail, enduring humiliation, defeat and estrangement in order to preserve more fully their vision of the inner reality of Irish possibilities. Hence their readiness and willingness "to sacrifice the body of Ireland for the soul" (*PI*, 81). The couple represent a line of last defense and make it synonymous with a new horizon. Through the jeopardy of their visionary isolation, they project renewal.

In the same spirit, *Try the Sky* concludes with the protagonist, Jose, returning to Ireland with his mistress Carlotta after numerous continental viccissitudes. They travel back in an aircraft named *Spirit,* and their return is the apotheosis of a joint dedication to the future. Jose experiences his return as follows:

> Something was going on inside me, deep and disturbing. As though the atmosphere of my own country, austere and unearthly behind its mask of gloom and dilapidation, was taking possession of me. . . . O Ireland! O Carlotta! O Love! . . . You are my heaven, you three together.[15]

Heaven consists of a severe and uncontaminated embodiment of romance. Tutored by Carlotta in facing "all the useless, inexplicable lonely suffering of the world" (*TTS,* 29), Jose ends up equipped to resume relations with his native place. Previously, "to go back now would be to leave half of myself behind" (*TTS,* 24). Having witnessed Carlotta's embodiment of sacrifice and ardent spiritual hunger, however, Jose is enabled to negotiate anew, and more completely, the land of his birth.

Stuart's insistence on tenacity, on taking extreme positions, on going all the way, on revaluing values, on archetype and prototype, and on the desirability of spiritual commitment, make his novels of the thirties re-petitive and predictable. All seem chapters in a prolonged romance, or perhaps a dream, about the ideology of egoism. Each of them is structured around incidents and motifs of rejection and reclamation, isolation and restitution, deprivation and reward. Yet despite their many longeurs of style, characterization and narrative, they convey quite unpredictably and persuasively the neuraesthenia of the quest, romance's fundamental premise. The ordeal of Garry Delea in *The Coloured Dome*—what he describes as "the secret pilgrimage of self-oblation"[16]—is intended to be reinvigorating and exemplary, as well as obligatory. To lose oneself is to find one's proper country. To drop out is to find a more valuable point of reentry. To dissent is to affirm.

Spirit, integrity, singleness-crystallizations of self, generally speaking—are what Stuart's novels (early and late) uphold. The Stuart protagonists's separation of himself from daily life leads to a broadening of his spiritual, psychic, and emotional experience, resulting in a more profound, more sympathetic, more central acquaintance with a world that is no longer merely diurnal.

Primacy of self is also a fundamental issue in Denis Devlin's verse, as Samuel Beckett has noted: "With himself on behalf of himself, with his selves on behalf of his selves. Tour d'ébène."[17] But the outcome of this commitment is rather different from Stuart's projections which, by comparison, may be said to aspire to a "tour d'ivoire." In Devlin's case, there is no culminating expression of a generic, exemplary self. On the contrary, Beckett notes, Devlin's verse arises out of "the need that is the absolute predicament of particular human identity," out of a sense of the insoluble, the incomplete: "My death is my life's plumed gnomon."[18] The project in Stuart's *The Coloured Dome*—"Making a harmony out of the irresponsible prodigality of life" (*TCD*, 91)—is not available to the passionate, severe, fastidious intelligence at work in Devlin's poetry. The verse's triumph is to articulate the irony of prodigality rather than to assert the romance of harmony:

> Magnificence, this terse-lit, star-quartz universe,
> Woe, waste and magnificence, my soul!
> ("Meditation at Avila," *CP,* 53)

Devlin's poetry is the totality of that irony at play in all seriousness.

In many ways, Denis Devlin seems to be very different from Stuart. His cultural background is Dublin Catholic (though he was born in Greenock, Scotland, in 1908), and his education resembles Joyce's to some extent: secondary education at Belvedere College, followed by degrees from University College, Dublin (after a decision to abandon training for the priesthood). Further study at Munich and Paris led eventually to a career in the Irish diplomatic corps, with postings to, among other places, Rome, New York and Washington. In 1958 he was appointed Ambassador to Italy. He died in 1959.

Devlin is unlike Stuart, too, in his devotion to literature (Stuart's interests are ultimately less aesthetic than ideological), both in the bookishness of his verse and as a translator, particularly of St. John Perse ("perhaps Perse's best translator").[19] Indeed, there is in Devlin's verse a feature which T. S. Eliot found in Perse's:

> The reader has to allow the images to fall into his memory successively without questioning the reasonableness of each at the moment; so that, at the end, a total effect is produced.[20]

Partly because of its range, partly because of its modernity, partly because of the compressed energy of its imaginative commitment, it is tempting to agree that:

Devlin seems un-Irish (not anti-) and certainly not English, he is rather a European. . . . Many of the poems have "Irish" subjects, but . . . there are almost no traces of Yeats's "romantic Ireland."[21]

Yet Devlin does share some common ground with Stuart. They both appeal to the realm of the spirit, both regard love as the vital crux in human affairs; neither shies away from the imponderable, the abstract, the metaphysical. And one of Devlin's selves is, like Stuart, very much preoccupied with questions of cultural identity:

> Divinities of my youth,
> Expounged to me my truth;
> Whether from Judah or Rome
> Or my nearer Gaeldom.
>
> ("The Colours of Love," *CP*, 20)

Since Devlin's verse is a matrix of psychic probes and spiritual meditations it is difficult and misguided to distinguish a specific concern with contemporary Irish culture from the poet's larger metaphysical urgencies. Even a poem on an explicitly Irish subject, "The Death of Michael Collins" (in honor of the organizational genius of the Irish War of Independence), purges the event of its historical aspects and enlarges its human significance: "Most I remember him, how man is courage." And the poem ends by quietly asserting the remedial, honorific, integrative powers of verse:

> Walking to Vespers in my Jesuit school,
> The sky was come and gone: 'O Captain, my Captain!'
> Walt Whitman was the lesson that afternoon—
> How sometimes death magnifies him who dies,
> And some, though mortal, have achieved their race.
>
> (*CP*, 17)

By means of verse, Collins's death is a rebirth on a higher plane. His people have lost him and retain him. The standard attainment of elegy is here a metaphor for Devlin's poetic vision, an aesthetic of absence as restitution, of incompleteness as a redemptive reality. Or, as "The Colours of Love" has it:

> It cannot well be said of love and death
> That love is better and that death is worse,
> Unless we buy death off with loving breath
> So he may rent his beauty with our purse.
>
> But is that beauty, is that beauty death?
> No, it's the mask by which we're drawn to him,
> It is with our consent death finds his breath;
> Love is death's beauty and annexes him.
>
> (*CP*, 19)

Devlin's project is to admit to his verse the "other" identified, but not apprehended, in "The Heavenly Foreigner":

> Something there was other
> Always at my elbow,
> I sang, hunted and hated one;
> He sings and hunts and hates me;
> Say heaven or hell
> Well or ill
> I cannot make it different,
> Anything, or even other.

What his friend, the poet and critic Brian Coffey, has called "the central element in Devlin's poetic activity" is "his aim and search for what is most distant, most different and most distinct from us humans, and his attempt to bring that most distant beyond all sensible or imagined horizons into human proximity."[22]

Devlin's "Lough Derg" provides a precise cultural context for "his aim and search." The title refers to Saint Patrick's Purgatory, off the northwest coast, Ireland's most celebrated place of pilgrimage, which has received literary attention from, among many others, Dante, Calderón and Seamus Heaney. Devlin, who comes closer to being an authentically religious poet—that is, a poet of faith—than any other modern Irish poet, meditates on the religion of his fellow-countrymen and on the heritage of the Irish Church. The highly allusive and syntactically curt rhythms of the poem make it a monument to the problematic character of its subject. Its manner enacts its matter: do modes of apprehension underwrite misgiving or belief? Witness the present age, in which

> Not all
>
> The men of God nor the priests of mankind
> Can men or explain the good and broke, not one
> Generous with love prove communion.
>
> (CP, 37)

The poet's pilgrimage takes a path higher than, but parallel to his people's, to whom,

> All is simple, and symbol in their world,
> The incomprehended rendered fabulous.
>
> (CP, 35)

And he castigates the narrowness of their faith ("Clan Jansen!") and finds in their expression of it and in the pilgrimage as a form of affirmation, occasion for incredulity:

With mullioned Europe shattered, this Northwest,
Rude-sainted Isle would pray it whole again:
(Peasant Apollo! Troy is worn to rest.)
Europe that humanized the sacred bane
Of God's chance who yet laughed in his mind
And balanced thief and saint: were they this kind?

(*CP,* 35)

In the light of the recent barbarisms and incoherencies of European history (the poem was published in 1946), Lough Derg seems a hopelessly inadequate last outpost. It is a place of incongruous fidelity and devotion, in a world where the heritage enshrining such options is in collapse, defaced, exhausted. Yet in the very act of satisfying the case rejecting his people's model of metaphysical witnessing (Devlin's verse in general is vivified by the will and tension of argument), the poet is drawn, as so often, to counteract what seems to be finality. The poem ends by combining philosophic remoteness and circumstantial closeness, as though it were itself a pilgrimage ending in the problematical renewal of partial illumination and ironical testament:

We pray to ourself. The metal moon, unspent
Virgin eternity sleeping in the mind,
Excites the form of prayer without content;
Whitehorn lightens, delicate and blind,
The negro mountain, and so, knelt upon her sod,
This woman beside me murmuring, *My God! My God!*

(*CP,* 38)

In "Lough Derg," Devlin approaches his heritage from a distance of which he is perhaps all too conscious. Nevertheless the approach is made, and comprehension is articulated in terms of a rift between poet and pretext. Yet even here, a rite of separation and return is evident. And in the enactment of the ritual, we find again (as in his "The Passion of Christ") the jeopardy into which all of Devlin's verse enters:

Let us take on the whole
Story in its negligence and passion.

(*CP,* 8)

—his mind's ardor ceaselessly polishing allotropes of incompleteness.

3

The typical movement in Stuart's and Devlin's work is from outside inward, from displacement to attempted accommodation. In the case of

Flann O'Brien and Thomas Kinsella, the movement goes the opposite way. Possibly because neither writer became an exile in a geographical sense (in fact, both had successful careers in the Irish Civil Service), there is a controlled sense of disruption or irruption in their work, in contrast to the motifs of intervention and reconciliation typical of Devlin and Stuart. Perhaps as a corollary, O'Brien's satire supplants Stuart's romance, while for Kinsella, cultural discontinuity synopsises the epistemology of metaphysical disquiet which Devlin's verse encodes. Yet, despite a difference in trajectory, the operation of the movement remains constant. O'Brien and Kinsella, no less than their predecessors, absent themselves in order to redeem. For them, too, the text is a saving grace.

Flann O'Brien is the pseudonym of Brian O'Nolan, a native of county Tyrone but a thorough Dubliner since his student days at University College, Dublin, where he concluded his studies with an M.A. dissertation on modern Irish poetry. A career civil servant in the Department of Local Government, his literary reputation rests on three novels: *At Swim-Two-Birds, The Third Policeman* and *The Poor Mouth*. In addition to and arguably surpassing O'Brien's literary reputation is his reputation as a satirical journalist, based on a column entitled "Cruiscin Lán" (Irish for "full little jug"), which appeared in *The Irish Times* newspaper under the pseudonym Myles na gCopaleen, from 1960 to 1966.

O'Brien's enactment of the movement occurs in the opening sentence of his first novel:

> Having placed in my mouth sufficient bread for three minutes' chewing, I withdrew my powers of sensual perception and retired into the privacy of my mind, my eyes and face assuming a vacant and preoccupied expression. I reflected on the subject of my spare-time literary activities. One beginning and one ending for a book was a thing I did not agree with.[23]

Mind has no necessary connection with mastication. Behind the aphasiac's demeanor the imagination has free play. And the novel proceeds to subject the idea of literary form and the existence of literary tradition to a marvellously inventive critique. The student-narrator (a non-Dedalus if ever there was one) propounds his markedly non-Dedalian—in other words, informal—theory of literature as follows to his friend Brinsley:

> In replying to an inquiry, it was explained that a satisfactory novel should be a self-evident sham to which the reader could regulate at will the degree of his credulity. It was undemocratic to compel characters to be uniformly good or bad, or poor or rich. Each should be allowed a private life, self-determination and a decent standard of living. This would make for self-respect, contentment and better service. It would be incorrect to say that it would lead to chaos. Characters should be interchangeable as

between one book and another. The entire corpus of existing literature should be regarded as a limbo from which discerning authors could draw their characters as required, creating only when they failed to find a suitable existing puppet. The modern novel should be largely a work of reference. (*ASTB*, 25)

The polyvalence of heritage disorders forms and kinds. Thus, in *At Swim-Two-Birds* we find cowboys consorting with fairy-folk. Translations of piercing simplicity of the Middle Irish romance, *Buile Suibhne*, occur in close proximity to the dead doggerel of one of the novel's characters, Jem Casey, proletarian poet. Characters in one of the three plots conspire to kill that plot's (fictional) author. From these and numerous other literary japes, there is plenty of evidence to support one of the author's concluding assertions: "Evil is even, truth is an odd number" (*ASTB*, 216). This novel is also notable for O'Brien's obvious relish in striking out against the boredom of finality. His ambition is to install the imagination as an autonomous agency, whose value derives from its authorization of whimsy, unevenness, the necessarily unforeseeable and unsummable, the definitive indivisibility of whole (odd) numbers.

From literature as such, O'Brien's novels go on to undermine, in turn, intellectual endeavour generally considered *(The Third Policeman)*[24] and cultural politics, narrowly considered *(The Poor Mouth)*.[25] In the former, which is by far the more sophisticated and unsettling achievement of the two, the notional stability proposed by theory, the obsessiveness of pedantic scholarship, the blandishments of taxonomical imperatives—all disintegrate under the insistence of the author's imaginative subversion. By means too elaborate to describe here, O'Brien suspends the motion of time and creates spatial disorientation. Matter loses its stability (one of the novel's best-known jokes is a strictly articulated argument to the effect that bicycles may turn into their owners and vice versa). Objects defy perceptibility ("It took me hours of thought long afterwards to realize why these articles were astonishing. They lacked an essential property of all known objects. . . . I can only say that these objects, not one of which resembled the other, were of no known dimensions." *TTP*, 135) And in the figure of de Selby, the philosopher to whom the narrator rather gruesomely and amorally devotes his life, O'Brien subverts limits, definitions, logic—a whole epistemology of knowledge as value, in effect.

Had *The Third Policeman* been published at the time of its completion, the sting of a remark made by O'Brien in 1945 would probably have been more acute: "Is it not time that you Irish woke up to the unsuspected frailty of the human intellect?"[26] By 1945, however, the original of *The Poor Mouth* had revealed the specifically Irish targets of O'Brien's satirical artillery. Here his aim is directed at the state of the Irish language and at the degraded social conditions of so-called native speakers. The exposure of official hypocrisy and incompetence is unsparing. Efforts to cherish and rehabilitate Irish are demolished for being based on unreflecting sentimentality and for being totally devoid of common sense. The ideal of rehabilitation lives in the past; the objects of its implementation exist in the present. The more ardent the ideal, the more punitive and irrelevant its implementation. And despite the subject's limited appeal, here too O'Brien's complex sense of heritage, his impatience with the status quo, and the animus that the thought of formal structures inspires in him are all devastatingly to the fore.

To conceive of the mind not in terms of disciplines but in terms of associations and to see the imagination not as a medium of interpretation but as a zone of autonomy that exists in defiance of orthodoxy and formality are perhaps a reminder of the aesthetic of *Finnegans Wake*. Despite Joyce's praise for *At Swim-Two-Birds* ("That's a real writer, with the true comic spirit. A really funny book")[27] his illustrious predecessor seemed to O'Brien to embody problems with which much of his own most inventive fiction is preoccupied, problems of continuity and flux. O'Brien criticized Joyce on the grounds that, "all his works, not excluding *Finnegans Wake*, have a rigid classic pattern."[28] Moreover, O'Brien's own imaginative commitments are unmediated by "vision," "conscience," or any such loftiness. An artist whose lack of egotism is one of his most noticeable characteristics, O'Brien ironically surrenders to the imagination. Yet despite his various misgivings about it, the example of Joyce's achievement—emphasizing as it does the purgative, the restorative and the faithful—apply equally well to O'Brien himself:

> Humour, handmaid of sorrow and fear, creeps out endlessly in all Joyce's works. He uses the thing . . . to attenuate the fear of those who have belief and who genuinely think that they will be in hell or in heaven shortly, and possibly very shortly. With laughs he palliates the sense of doom that is the heritage of the Irish Catholic. True humour needs this background urgency. . . . (*S&P*, 208)

Parody rectifies. Satire cleanses. Imaginative anarchism renews.

Thomas Kinsella's biography is as bare as his poetry is intense. Born and educated in Dublin, he abandoned his studies for a science degree to take up a career in the Ministry of Finance, and now supports himself by teaching, lecturing and writing.

Kinsella's early poetry expresses more forcefully the irruptive and disruptive movements of O'Brien's fiction:

> Sick of the piercing company of women
> I swung the gate shut with a furious sigh
> Rammed trembling hands in pockets and drew in
> A breath of river air.[29]

But while Kinsella's verse can be as corrosively satirical as anything in the annals of either Flann O'Brien or Myles na gCopaleen, it also contains a powerful sense of broken-heartedness. The ego, the artistic inquiry before which O'Brien defers, here suffers the incompleteness that the poems aggressively bewail. In Kinsella's hands satire is not a demonstration of literariness; it is an instrument of surgery and of pain. Perhaps as a result, the broken, interrupted condition of the Irish cultural tradition is much more in evidence in Kinsella's verse than in O'Brien's fiction. "I am certain that a great part of the significance of my own past, as I try to write my poetry, is that that past is mutilated."[30] While in the same essay, speaking of his contemporaries, Kinsella describes himself: "I can learn nothing from them except that I am isolated."

The poet's working conditions, it seems, have an inevitable bias of remoteness. So, in the verse of "perhaps the most seriously talented Irish poet since Yeats"[31] there is a repeated sense of venturing out into and away from, negotiating distance rather than returning from it. As "Downstream" has it: "Searching the darkness for a landing place" (SP, 59). In all of Kinsella's work, there is an urgent metaphysic of passage. And accompanying the sense of fractured culture is a stronger sense of time's more personal ravages, expressed by the fragility of love and the ironclad fact of death. Thus, "Phoenix Park," one of the poet's most elaborate dramatic meditations (formally, Kinsella's verse owes much to the dramatic lyric, except that the drama is internal, pychic, private) opens: "One stays or leaves. The one who returns is not / The one, etcetera. And we are leaving" (SP 101). In his oeuvre's more frequent encounters with death, passage, departure, and absence are made all the more undeniable, as in "Cover her Face":

> I watch her drift, in doubt whether dead or born
> · · · · · · · · · · · · · · · · · ·
>   out of the worn
> Bulk of day, under its sightless eye,
> And close her dream in hunger. So we die.
>
>   (SP, 48)

From such confrontations, from a poet who so comprehensively repudiates the mask, it should come as no surprise to find, in "Baggot Street Deserta":

> Versing, like an exile, makes
> A virtuoso of the heart,
> Interpreting the old mistakes
> And discords in a work of Art
> For the One, a private masterpiece
> Of doctored recollections.
>
>   (SP, 48)

The interpenetration of personal and public, of cultural and psychological, is impressively enacted in "Nightwalker," a poem of pilgrimage, whose object is also reconciliation through exposure. To characterize the end of the poem's unnerving stroll as "I think this is the Sea of Disappointment" represents in this context an act of confrontation along the lines set forth in "Baggot Street Deserta":

> A voice clarifies when the tingle
> Dies out along the nerves of time:
> *Endure and let the present punish.*
>
> (*SP,* 27)

The Sea of Disappointment is a location echoing lunar geography: the poem opens with a rejection of the moon's symbolic appeal ("Moron voiceless moon. / That dark area, the mark of Cain.") In this, as in other respects—even perhaps in its fragmentary prosody—the poem offers a querulous challenge to Yeats. (One of the most obvious of these respects, culturally speaking, is the provision of "Joyce's Martello Tower" as a venue for the speaker's lacerating deliberations of contemporary Irish politics.)

The poem's satiric verve may be savored from the following lines, whose origin, biographically speaking, is Kinsella's civil service years:

> All about and above me
> The officials on the corridors or in their rooms
> Work, or overwork, with mixed motives
> Or none. We dwell together in urgency;
> Dominate, entering middle age; subserve,
> Aborting vague tendencies with buttery smiles.
> Among us, behind locked doors, the ministers
> Are working, with a sureness of touch found early
> In the nation's birth—the blood of enemies
> And brothers dried on their hide long ago.
> Dragon old men, upright and stately and blind,
> Or shuffling in the corridor finding a key,
> Their youth cannot die in them; it will be found
> Beating with violence when their bodies rot.
>
> (*SP,* 89)

Yet for all "Nightwalker's" stinging excoriation, there are constant references to "we," "my people," "our," "our neighbours." As the speaker admits, he not only sees his subject, he is of it:

> I stroll upon my way, a vagabond
> Tethered.
>
> (*SP,* 87)

And if all that offers itself for contemplation are

> Spirit-skeletons . . . straggling into view
> From the day's depths

one accepts:

> You can pick them out
> In the night sky, with a little patience.

(*SP,* 89)

   Implicitly, such "patience" is part of the poet's abiding by his subject, the counterpart to spleen.
   Patience, however, only obtains in the wake of travail. In order for its deployment to be effective, the ordeal of estrangement must be undergone. An aesthetic of abiding arises out of a metaphysic of departure. Breakdown has to be authenticated to permit of a saving grace. In these terms, perhaps the most potent image that Kinsella's verse provides of his condition are contained in the closing lines of "Baggot Street Deserta." The poet looks out on his world from the window of his room (the location a provocatively lower middle-class tower):

> Fingers cold against the sill
> Feel, below the stress of my flight
> The slow implosion of my pulse
> In a wrist with poet's cramp, a tight
> Beat tapping out endless calls
> Into the dark, as the alien
> Garrison in my own blood
> Keeps constant contact with the main
> Mystery, not to be understood.
> Out where imagination arches
> Chilly points of light transact
> The business of the border-marches
> Of the Real, and I—a fact
> That may be countered or may not—
> Find their privacy complete.
>
> My quarter-inch of cigarett
> Goes flaring down to Baggot Street.

(*SP,* 28)

Attached and remote, involuntary but willingly, the poet allows his optic to work on him, and discharges himself through it. "Nightwalker" again:

> Clean bricks
> Are made of mud; we need them for our tower.

(*SP,* 88)

4

As suggested at the outset exile is a movement of the mind, a cultural reaction, a metonym for the restlessness, disaffection, isolation, and self-respect for the aesthetically or spiritually committed Irish writer in the years since the granting of Irish independence. The term connotes a shared characteristic, a collective gesture, variously embodied but consistently utilized. Clearly, the term is far from being the last word, on either the writers using it or the conditions that gave rise to their work.

In the case of the two writers discussed who are still living, the work of rehabilitation goes on. Stuart has produced his definitive statement in *Black List Section H* (1971), a novel recounting in very loosely fictional form the events of his life up to and including the end of his wartime sojourn in Nazi Germany. His reemergence as an unironical spokesman for cultural values first rehearsed more than fifty years ago has stimulated Irish literary life in recent years ("It is only those few writers capable of imagining alternative societies who can enter into a serious and naturally advantageous relationship with their own").[32]

Kinsella, on the other hand, has persistently advanced the claims of a more far-ranging concept of continuity. Throughout his career he has attempted to voice a silenced heritage, literature in Irish. His translations of both saga materials (*The Táin*, 1969) and poems written between 1600 and 1900 (*An Duanaire,* with Seán O Tauma, 1981) testify to this redemptive commitment.

Moreover, the movement sketched above may also be perceived in the work of writers who still await full international recognition: the novelist Aidan Higgins and the poet Derek Mahon. Both these authors carry the example—if not the aesthetic—of Beckett back to Irish writing. And while they cannot improve on Beckett's deployment of silence and exile, they achieve cunning and original descriptions of the movement that beset their predecessors. Higgins' sprawling, polyglot, uneven novel, *Balcony of Europe* (1975), is a case in point. As for Mahon, the following lines express one of his more enduring moods:

> Why am I always staring out
> Of windows, preferably from a height?
> . . . .
> Yet distance is the vital bond
> Between the window and the wind,
> While equilibrium demands
> A cold eye and deliberate hands.[33]

Exile lives, continuingly, at the heart of modern Irish writing; absenting, consenting. Paradoxical muse. "Old artificer . . ."

Notes

1. James Joyce, *A Portrait of the Artist as a Young Man,* ed. Chester Anderson (New York: Viking, 1968), p. 253. Cited hereafter in text as *P.*

2. James Joyce, *Selected Letters,* ed. Richard Ellmann (New York: Viking, 1975), p. 72. Cited hereafter in text as *SL.*

3. Thomas Flanagan, "Yeats, Joyce and the Matter of Ireland," *Critical Inquiry* 2 (Autumn 1975) 1:61.

4. W. B. Yeats, *Collected Poems* (London: Macmillan, 1967), p. 169. Cited hereafter in text, as *CP.*

5. W. B. Yeats, *Autobiographies* (London: Macmillan, 1955), pp. 253–54.

6. Richard Ellmann, *Yeats, The Man and the Masks* (London: Faber & Faber, 1961), p. 292.

7. Samuel Beckett, *All That Fall* (London: Faber & Faber, 1965), pp. 10–11.

8. W. B. Yeats, *Uncollected Prose,* vol. 2, eds. John P. Frayne and Colton Johnson (New York: Columbia University Press, 1976), pp. 438–39.

9. Yeats, *Autobiographies,* p. 97.

10. Terence Brown, *Ireland: Social and Cultural History 1922–1979* (London: Fontana, 1981) p. 41.

11. J. H. Natterstad, "Interview with Francis Stuart," *Journal of Irish Literature* 5, no. 1 (1976):22. Among Yeats's notes of generosity was praise for Stuart in a letter to Olivia Shakespeare: "Read *The Coloured Dome* by Francis Stuart. It is strange and exciting in theme and perhaps more personally and beautifully written than any other book of our generation; it makes you understand the strange Ireland that is rising up there." *Letters of W. B. Yeats,* ed. Allen Wade (London: Rupert Hart-Davis, 1954), pp. 799–800.

12. Francis Stuart, *Things to Live For, Notes for an Autobiography* (London: Jonathan Cape, 1934) p. 144. Cited hereafter in text as *TTLF.*

13. Natterstad, "Francis Stuart," p. 17.

14. Stuart, *Pigeon Irish* (New York: Macmillan, 1932), p. 37. Cited hereafter in text as *PI.*

15. Stuart, *Try the Sky* (London: Gollanez, 1933), p. 286. Cited hereafter in text as *TTS.*

16. Stuart, *The Coloured Dome* (New York: Macmillan, 1933), p. 263. Cited hereafter in text as *TCD.*

17. Samuel Beckett, *Disjecta,* ed. Ruby Cohn (New York: Grove Press, 1984), pp. 91–94.

18. Denis Devlin, *Collected Poems,* ed. Brian Coffey (Dublin: Dolmen Press, 1964). Cited hereafter in text as *CP.* The line quoted is from "Est Prodest," *CP,* 49.

19. Arthur Knodel, *St. John-Perse. A Study of His Poetry* (Edinburgh: Edinburgh University Press, 1966), p. 67.

20. T. S. Eliot, "Preface to *Anabasis,*" in *Selected Prose of T. S. Eliot,* ed. Frank Kermode (New York: Harcourt Brace Jovanovich/Farrar, Straus and Giroux, 1975), p. 77.

21. Tate, Allen, and Robert Penn Warren, "Preface" to Denis Devlin, *Selected Poems* (New York: Holt, Rinehart & Winston 1963), p. 14.

22. Brian Coffey, "Denis Devlin. Poet of Distance," in *Place, Personality and the Irish Writer* Andrew Carpenter, ed. (Gerrard's Cross: Colin Smyth, 1977), p. 151.

23. Flann O'Brien, *At Swim-Two-Birds* (London, 1939; Harmondsworth, Eng.: Penguin, 1967), p. 9. Cited hereafter in text as *ASTB.*

24. Flann O'Brien, *The Third Policeman* (London, 1939; rpt., London: Hart-Davis, MacGibbon, 1967). Cited hereafter in text as *TTP.* This novel was completed in 1940. O'Brien's other two novels, *The Dalkey Archive* (1964) and the *Hard Life* (1961) pale in comparison to their predecessors.

25. Originally in Irish as *An Béal Bocht* (Dublin: An Cló Náisiúnta 1941). *The Poor Mouth,* trans. Patrick C. Power (London: Hart-Davis, MacGibbon, 1973).

26. Quoted in Anne Clissmann, *Flann O'Brien. A Critical Introduction to His Writings* (Dublin: Gill & Macmillan, 1975), p. 356, n.19.

27. Clissmann, *Flann O'Brien* p. 79.

28. Flann O'Brien, "A Bash in the Tunnel," in his *Stories and Plays* (New York: Penguin, 1977), p. 207. Cited hereafter in text as *S&P.*

29. Thomas Kinsella, "A Country Walk," in *Selected Poems 1956–1968* (Dublin: Dolmen Press, 1973). Cited hereafter in text as *SP.*

30. Kinsella, "The Irish Writer," in *Davis, Mangan, Ferguson? Tradition and the Irish Writer,* Roger McHugh, ed. (Dublin: Dolmen Press, 1970), p. 66.

31. Calvin Bedient, *Eight Contemporary Poets* (London: Oxford University Press, 1974), p. 119.

32. Francis Stuart, "The Soft Center of Irish Writing," in *Paddy No More,* William Vorm, ed. (Dublin: Wolfhound Press, 1978), p. 5.

33. Derek Mahon, *Poems 1962–1978* (Oxford: Oxford University Press 1979), p. 112.

Exile in Heinrich Boell's Novel: *Billiards at Half Past Nine*

ROSMARIE T. MOREWEDGE

Political dissent and exile in Germany do not start in 1933 with opposition to National Socialism. Great German writers like Friedrich Schiller and Heinrich Heine had to write their major works in exile. Tragic though exile was for Heine, whose Parisian exile from Germany became both an existential mode and a literary theme, his exile and that of other writers of the Young Germans movement are not found under literary discussions of exile, for in German literature the term "exile" is by common consent reserved for those writers who felt compelled to leave Germany for political, racial, or other reasons between 1933 and 1945, i.e., during the rule of the totalitarian fascist regime of Hitler.[1]

The ascent of a dictatorial, repressive government in Germany, *Gleichschaltung* of all aspects of German life and letters, the proclamation of racial laws, the publication of blacklisted works and authors, the Nazi book burning of works by German-Jewish authors and others deemed to be in opposition to National Socialism, and the purge of the Prussian Academy of Art are some of the chief reasons for the exodus of thousands of writers and intellectuals from Germany to other countries willing to accept them.[2] Vienna, Prague, Zurich, Amsterdam, Denmark, Paris, Madrid, and other way stations served as temporary shelters for many until the eventual arrival of the fascists.[3] Although America was the preferred port of most exiled writers and intellectuals, many remained in Europe, hoping that the madness in Germany would come to a quick end. What a terrible disappointment when National Socialism spread to their temporary shelters in Europe! No fate was worse than to be turned over to the Nazi invaders by local

A shorter version of this essay was delivered as a paper in a lecture series on the theme of "Exile" sponsored by the Department of Romance Languages. I am grateful to Professor Sandro Sticca and Professor María-Inés Lagos-Pope for inviting me to make this presentation.

partisans. Yet safe passage to America was difficult to obtain because of numerous American immigration restrictions.[4] Once in exile, emigrants were cut off from their own language, culture, publishers, readers, critics, and friends.[5] Writers found survival difficult under the most favorable of circumstances. Those circumstances were more often than not less than favorable—if not downright hostile. United by little except their opposition to National Socialism, they could not be expected to put aside the *Weltanschauung* that was inextricably linked to the mode of their artistic production. Although it is certainly true that German writers in exile demonstrated a greater sense of cohesiveness than others who had left Germany for racial or other reasons, it must still be remembered that German writers did not and could not speak with one voice in host countries. Lion Feuchtwanger affirmed as much when he stated in his novel *Exil,* "Die deutsche Emigration war zerklüfteter als jede andere" ("The German emigration movement was more deeply fissured than any other").[6] Some respected spokesmen did emerge among the emigrants, most notably Thomas Mann in the United States, who gained great recognition for his courageous writings and broadcasts that fought National Socialism and offered spiritual support to those who opposed Hitler and fascism in Germany.[7]

Although most writers in exile soon broke off, or were forced to break off communications with a Germany they deemed to be wholly in the claws of the devil, news came to them of an underground in Germany. The presence of underground resistance movements to National Socialism within Germany was known to many writers in exile.[8] Occasionally works of resistance writers were even smuggled across the German borders—once, as in the noted case of Jan Petersen, in two loaves of bread. Opposition to National Socialism within Germany was expressed by German writers in many different ways as circumstances permitted.[9] Literary opposition to the Nazi rule is clearly documented for many writers who chose to stay in Germany or were unable to leave the country for financial or other reasons.[10] For some writers such resistance led to incarceration in concentration camps; for others it led to officially enforced silence, and for still others it led to an attitude of what has been called *innere Emigration—* spiritual exile, or inner emigration.[11] While distancing themselves from the totalitarian system they opposed for a variety of reasons, writers who had chosen inner emigration as a response to National Socialism typically expressed such opposition at least in some of their works, where fascism is not attacked directly, but under camouflage. Contemporary readings of such works by groups similarly opposed to National Socialism show that these publications—often novels, short stories, or poems—did reach a public that was able to read between the lines, a public able to discern between the allegorical, historical, or mythical cloak and the real subject matter: criticism of National Socialism. Although the effectiveness of the camouflage was, at times, introduced as evidence to suggest that this art was really not very different from National Socialist sponsored art, authorial intentions, the reception of the work by opponents of the regime, and often official censorship bear out that many works that were censored had been written by writers who claim to have distanced themselves ideologically from National Socialism.[12] One must remember that few other avenues of action were open to those opposed to National Socialism but unable—or even for certain reasons unwilling—to leave Germany. Direct criticism of the regime would undoubtedly have led to denial of permission to write, confiscation of all printed copies, concentration camp, or suicide.[13]

After the defeat of Hitler the so-called good Germans, who had left Germany when Hitler first came to power, were free to return to the land they had been forced to leave. While many did return, others preferred not to do so, and some even refused to return when they discovered that the Germans who had remained in Germany refused—on the whole—to accept responsibility for the atrocities committed by Germany from 1933 to 1945.[14] German intellectuals claimed to have resisted fascism, to have made no more than the necessary compromises to assure survival, and to have withdrawn into spiritual exile or silence when active opposition to National Socialism was tantamount to death. Self-appointed spokesmen for these intellectuals, such as Frank Thiess and others, claimed to have been the real sufferers. Had not writers like Thomas Mann been spared this suffering, while they watched the destruction of Germany passively from orchestra seats in safe and comfortable surroundings?[15] Those who had remained expected those who had gone into exile, whom they regarded as the more fortunate ones, to return and to heal the wounds of the less fortunate, who—so it was said—had found the courage to stay in Germany.[16] Their wounds, they claimed, were deep. Had they not endured the fire of the *Gestapo,* untold deprivation, censorship, suspicion, fear, surveillance, loss of contact with other writers, and some, like E. Wiechert, even the concentration camp? Had they not been forced to face death and dying in Germany on a regular basis? By contrast, had those who had been given the opportunity to leave the country not enjoyed freedom of self-expression, safety, and contact with cultural developments in the West? Did the scale of suffering not tip in favor of those who had remained?

Boxed into the prison of its own view of its past, each side defended its own position and the role it presumed to have played during the twelve years of Nazi rule. From defending its own stance, each side soon advanced to deprecating if not attacking the other. The controversy that ensued has been documented in the correspondence of Frank Thiess and Thomas Mann.[17] When Walter von Molo asked Thomas Mann to return to Germany and help Germans recover their humanity, Thiess published an open letter in which he cited his own inner emigration and that of other writers as evidence of moral backbone and bravery in Germany during the reign of National Socialism. He stressed that it had taken more courage to stay in Germany than to abandon this hell.[18] Feeling that insult had been added to injury, Thomas Mann responded as the spokesman of all political emigrants by bitterly indicting all writers who had stayed behind as Nazi writers. He called for the destruction of all literature produced between 1933 and 1945 in Germany, labeling it bad Nazi art.[19] The question that emerged from this acrimonious debate is one that continues to be debated: Do Germans who remained in Germany between 1933 and 1945 and claim to have opposed National Socialism possess the moral right to claim to have gone into spiritual exile and inner emigration? Should the term "exile," which implies physical exile, be extended to cover spiritual exile as well as ideological and intellectual isolation in Germany? Were there really "good Germans," i.e., Germans who opposed National Socialism in Germany during 1933 to 1945? Or was all of Germany a nation gone to the devil that should be punished collectively for its atrocities by the victorious allies and those who had gone into physical exile and had returned as judges with victorious occupational forces? There were those, like F. Schonauer, E. Ludwig, and even Thomas Mann at one time, who judged all Germans collectively guilty.[20] Thomas Mann was even ready to put the axe to all of the so-called German Nazi art, equating it with the entire artistic output under Nazi rule. There were others—writers and critics—who felt that the literary and cultural output in Germany from 1933 to 1945 could not be judged by the yardstick of collective guilt and be found automatically wanting.[21] They argued—and in my opinion—rather convincingly—that unmistakable literary opposition had been expressed to fascism, tyranny, and Hitler in Germany during the reign of Hitler by writers who had not only distanced themselves intellectually, spiritually, and ideologically from fascism, but had expressed this opposition covertly, since open opposition would have led to certain death. They point to different forms of resistance, such as that of Wiechert at Buchenwald, who wrote his *Totenwald* (*Forest of the Dead*) as a result of his suffering and that of other inmates of the concentration camp. They point to satirical presentations of National Socialism. They point to writers, such as Ricarda Huch, who voluntarily left the Prussian Academy of Art and who published in Switzerland rather than in Germany; they claim that camouflage of real intent and real content was necessary and effective in concealing from Nazi censors but revealing to those in sympathy with the resistance movement criticism of and opposition to National Socialism. They point to official Nazi records that document censure or blacklisting of many publications because of perceived anti-Nazi intent, expression, and/or reception.[22] They point out that the humane spirit and encouraging message of many works were meant to support "good Germans" who, though silent, were opposed to National Socialism. These Germans needed such encouragement if they were to be able to hold out until National Socialism would finally be vanquished. While these critics and historians of literature do not support the unqualified inclusion of all writers writing in Germany between 1933 and 1945 under the rubric of *innere Emigration,* as Karl August Horst would have us do,[23] they eloquently document an opposition to fascism that took many forms and was read as such by a community of readers that was similarly opposed to fascism.[24] Many of those writers identified as part of this opposition argue persuasively that they made no more than minimal concessions to National Socialism while in inner emigration. They point out, with some justification, that not every writer opposed to fascism actually had the opportunity to go into exile.

If exile is defined as the voluntary emigration of single individuals or groups into a distant country as a consequence of economic, political, religious, and racial reasons that allow the victim only the choice of death or departure, then one cannot really speak of *innere Emigration* and had best abolish the term altogether, as W. A. Berendsohn and others have recommended.[25] If, however, one uses a looser definition, which allows us to accept voluntary departure and emigration into countries near or far for other reasons including intellectual alienation, then it is also possible to define *innere Emigration.*[26] With Charles Hoffmann I should like to define it as the attitude of writers who felt no longer at home in their native country (i.e., Germany or in countries under German control), either because of official disapproval or because of their own convictions.[27] The alienation they felt should not be interpreted as an aesthetic judgment or as a form of literary criticism. It is appropriate only as an expression of a certain attitude to National Socialism.

As was observed earlier, when the victorious occupational forces marched into a vanquished Germany, they expected to find a nation of National Socialists that had to be punished for its actions.[28] To their surprise they found few who actually acknowledged any kind of allegiance to or complicity with National Socialism. Ignorance, misunderstanding, or lack of responsibility was claimed by most; passive resistance and spiritual opposition to fascism was claimed by some, especially writers who asserted that they had withdrawn from an arena in which they felt alienated into the self. Some critics, as has been mentioned, went so far as to suggest that all writing under National Socialism should be presumed to have lived in spiritual exile.[29] Almost all intellectuals and writers defending their past claimed to have been "good Germans."

★   ★   ★

The Nobel Prize winner Heinrich Boell compels us to examine these and related issues in his novel *Billiards at Half Past Nine.*[30] Written in 1959 by an author who had been forced to participate in World War II as a soldier, even though at the onset he was still in his teens, the novel examines the fortunes of three generations of the Faehmel family during a fifty-one year period, stressing the years under National Socialism and the postwar years. Instead of dealing with writers, that is, with builders of the intellect, the novel deals with builders of concrete and steel, that is, with a family of architects. The Faehmel family is closely linked to and active in the building as well as the destruction of Germany; the problems and fortunes that beset the family stand symbolically for the problems besetting Germany during the years from 1907 to 1958. The novel explores in retrospect how each member of this prosperous, creative, industrious, intellectual, and politically aware family responded to National Socialism. Their response is meant to be understood as representative of that of many German families rather high on the socioeconomic ladder. The reaction within this family ranges from enthusiastic support for National Socialism to resistance to this totalitarian government, a resistance that entails inner emigration or inner exile for some members and physical exile into another country for others. While political positions emerge clearly, the lines separating one form of exile from another are not sharply drawn. It is appropriate to sketch the context that led to such different responses to fascism before we explore the meaning of exile within this novel.

Heinrich Faehmel, the founder of the Faehmel family, establishes himself as major architect, public-minded citizen, and family father during World War I and the years of the Weimar Republic, when architects and architecture played a key role in the Bauhaus movement. In the fashion advocated by Luther, which historically was upheld in Germany, he renders publicly unto Caesar what is Caesar's, even though he disapproves privately of Caesar.[31] Publicly he fulfills the social, political expectations made concerning members of his class, except for irrelevant eccentricities meant to enhance his image, distinguish him from the faceless crowd, and build a legend; privately he laughs about these expectations with ironic detachment.[32] While such moral and political schizophrenia may appear superficially harmless enough, and while Heinrich Faehmel is conscious of no negative consequences that resulted from such moral bifurcation, it is of tragic consequence for the upbringing of his two sons, Otto and Robert, one of whom comes to support with heart and soul those actions for which his father had received public honors,[33] while the other comes to support and identify himself with the disdain which the father had shown privately for actions that had received the public accolade.[34] The double fabric of Heinrich Faehmel's life produces two sons as unlike one another as night and day. One becomes the friend of political gangsters; the other risks his life to kill those gangsters.

Who is Heinrich Faehmel's wife and the mother of these two sons? It is Johanna Faehmel, who is incapable of moral double-dealing and who manages to stay out of prison only because as a woman she rarely has the occasion to act or express herself in public. In expressing openly what Mr. Faehmel thinks privately, she functions as his alter ego.

> It was Johanna who said right out what I'd been privately thinking. (81)
>
> . . . I didn't say what I should have, that is, that I agreed with her one hundred per cent. . . . All along I knew I should have been saying, "I agree with my wife, absolutely." I knew that irony wasn't enough, and never would be. (82)[35]

In spite of the chain of three *K*'s around her neck (*Kinder, Kirche, Küche*), she has to be declared insane twice (emotionally overwrought the first time) to deflect punishment from her for forthright public opposition to German militarism under absolutism on the one hand and National Socialism on the other. When Germany went increasingly mad under Hitler, she went into the insane asylum with the blessing of her family, so as to escape the otherwise certain death her political outspokenness would have brought about. Her life in the insane asylum during the Hitler and postwar years assumes the form of an exile for her—spiritual, intellectual, temporal, and physical.

> I know there's one way to give the murderers the slip—be certified insane. (139)
>
> . . . be quiet, old man, don't cry, I'm just living in inner emigration. . . . (141)[36]

The Faehmel offspring, Otto and Robert, receive from the parents qualities that allow the political National Socialist spark to catch fire on the one hand and the apolitical, ironic detachment to develop on the other. Otto, the obedient, social, gregarious, emotional, good-hearted boy becomes a gangster when he falls in with a band of political gangsters. Political blackmail of his parents is not too ugly a tool for him. Once close to political power, he becomes an unrecognizable shell of his former self to his parents, who quiver in fear of him, lest he turn them over to the *Gestapo* for sending money to an enemy of the state—their other son, who fled from Germany to escape certain death.

Robert, the reflective, polite, aloof, asocial thinker becomes involved with an underground group of political resisters mainly because of his moral single-mindedness, which does not allow him to tolerate the torture of defenseless human beings without coming to their aid. When members of this group attempt an unsuccessful political assassination, Robert barely escapes death for his presumed contribution. He and his companion Schrella manage to escape to Amsterdam, where he lives for several years in exile from Germany, until his mother finds it possible to effect through personal contacts his safe return.

Upon Robert's return it is evident that the unity of the Faehmel home has been torn to shreds because the family is openly divided along political lines. With the exception of the National Socialist Otto, all members of the family show their opposition to fascism in various degrees. Opposition to National Socialism, which, if openly expressed, would have led to the concentration camp, is seen in actions, such as Johanna Faehmel's attempt to share the fate of Jews who are being hauled off to concentration camps, her openly expressed empathy with political victims, and refusal to enjoy the advantages of her class (an enjoyment that made it possible for others of her class to pretend that war was not so bad after all), her break with a clergy that supported Hitler, and her eventual decision to take refuge in an insane asylum (2 May 1942), where euthanasia might occur at any moment. When she can neither tolerate the political horror around her nor lessen it without endangering her entire family, she withdraws spiritually into what she calls *innere Emigration*. It is significant that she withdraws into an insane asylum, for it is the looney bin that comes to stand symbolically for Germany, a country gone mad under Hitler. Separation from all that is dear to her and from reality is the price she pays for this exile, which is meant to protect her and her family. Hermetically, almost magically sealed off from life and from the flow of real time, she is free to express her political eccentricities where these no longer matter.

When Robert returns from exile to Germany and his family, which has now expanded to include his wife and child, he decides to go along with external political demands made of him while attempting to preserve his internal freedom to remain detached from organized political life. In compliance with the terms by which his return had been obtained, he joins Hitler's army as an officer upon finishing his study of statics. Unlike his father, who had also been a military officer but had offered nothing but private, intellectual resistance to absolutism and later to totalitarianism, Robert Faehmel uses his position as an officer of the army to express his own political opposition to National Socialism by waging his own war on Germany. He avenges the death of victims of Nazi torture by attacking Nazi culture. As the demolition expert of a mad Nazi general, he and those working with him proceed to destroy as many German cultural monuments as possible in memory of victims of Nazi torture, the real moral heroes under National Socialism in whose honor no monuments were built. At the end of the war he becomes a prisoner of war of the American forces; upon his return to Germany he withdraws into isolation and silence when he perceives that those who are building the New Germany are identical with those who created the old National Socialist Germany. Because of his perception that the new "democratic" Germany is but a repetition of the old militaristic Germany in which absolutism had after a short interlude been replaced by totalitarianism, a system of government not very different from absolutism, Robert Faehmel refuses to become reconciled to the New

Germany and its institutions, which embraced Hitler and democracy with equal ease.

> "I won't come to the consecration," thought Robert, "for I'm not reconciled. Not reconciled with the powers guilty of Ferdi's death, or with the ones that caused Edith to die and St. Severin's to be spared. I'm not reconciled, not reconciled either to myself or to the spirit of reconciliation which you in your official speech will proclaim. Blind passion did not destroy your home, hatred destroyed it, which was not blind and does not as yet repent. Should I confess it was I who did it? I'd have to inflict pain on my father, although he is not guilty, and perhaps on my son, although he is not guilty either, and on you, Reverend Father, although you, too, are not guilty; just who is guilty, then? I am not reconciled to a world in which a gesture or a word misunderstood can cost a life." And aloud he said, "Thank you very much, Reverend Father, it will give me great pleasure to attend your ceremony." (209)[37]

His alienation from Germany is most visible in his alienation from everyone in his own family and his refusal to be accessible to anyone outside his family and Schrella—except by mail.

Opposing what this New Germany stands for, he withdraws spiritually and intellectually into the world of abstractions and games he constructed for himself when he found reality wanting. His opposition to the restoration of the old order and its institutions is most evident in the billiard game. At a time when most self-respecting Germans have just begun their work day, when the office momentum reaches its first peak of intensity, Robert Faehmel has concluded his work for the day—one hour's worth, to be exact—and has initiated his play period at the Hotel Prince Heinrich. At this hotel, where his father had played billiards in the evening after work with officers of the army to affirm and strengthen his social status, Robert Faehmel's strange way of playing billiards in the company of Hugo, a young hotel employee, appears suspicious enough to the hotel porter to call for a character investigation. By scheduling his play period from 9:30 A.M. to 11 A.M., a time when others initiate their most intense work period, Robert Faehmel questions the entire German work ethos of building and rebuilding, as well as the concept of duty operative in German society—to which by common consent all free play has been subordinated and which excludes all free play that does not conform to socially recognized rules of loss and gain. Johanna Faehmel explains these social expectations as follows:

> Death . . . lurked in the eyes of the men to whom I would be thrown. Wearers of caps, guarders of the law. One thing only was forbidden: to want to live and play. Do you understand me, old man? Play was a deadly sin. Not sport, they put up with that, it kept you lively, made you graceful, pretty, and stimulated their wolfish appetite. Dolls' houses: good, they were all for housewifely and motherly instincts. Dancing: that

was good, too, part of the marriage market. But if I wanted to dance just to please myself up in my room in my petticoat, that was a sin because it wasn't a duty. . . . And I prayed for him, the one who would set me free and save me from death in the wolves lair. (139)[38]

By refusing to see Nettlinger when this opportunist makes the attempt to speak to Robert Faehmel during a billiard game at the hotel, Robert re-affirms his contempt for and opposition to the New German democracy, whose leaders held positions of responsibility under National Socialism. He does not believe that the denazification program has transformed former Nazis into "democrats by conviction."[39] But is his passive political opposition effective? Apparently not, at least not until Robert's political stance is interpreted to the insensitive Nettlinger by the returnee Schrella as an act of contempt for the new democrats and clear political opposition to the new democratic, allegedly denazified Germany.

"I'd be sorry if you thought I doubted the sincerity of your motives and feelings," Schrella said [to Nettlinger]. "I don't even doubt your remorse, but pictures—since you asked me to put the anecdote in my collection—involve an abstract idea, namely the part you played then, the part you play today. The parts—forgive me—are the same, because then the way to keep me harmless was to lock me up, whereas today the way to keep me harmless is to set me free. I'm afraid that's why Robert, who has more of an abstract mind than I have, doesn't care to meet you. (163)[40]

Instead of observing the rules of the billiard game, Robert Faehmel ignores them totally. In the act of playing he transforms the green field of the billiard table into a tensive field of abstractions, whose force, stress, and strain are explored within the narrative.[41] The game leads also to his perception of his arrest in time and the need to be redeemed from this suspension in time.[42] Most important, however, is the fact that playing billiards becomes an activity that allows the narrating ego to constitute itself through reminiscences, interior monologues, and conscious probing into the past as the past is narrated. That such self-constitution is an outcome of the billiard game is evident when it leads Robert Faehmel to reassume the "shepherd" role when he adopts Hugo as his son, a boy whose intellectual and personal development had been stunted by institutions that had learned to exploit and market his innocence and vulnerability effectively.

It is evident from the foregoing that Robert Faehmel's attitude of opposition, initially to National Socialism and subsequently to the New Germany, has not changed. His early physical exile in Amsterdam and his later spiritual exile from National Socialism as an officer during the war have left permanent scars on him. Earlier forms of exile have furnished the structure for his life in postwar Germany, where such exile is not, but should be unnecessary, since democracy is generally thought to tolerate if not thrive on dissent. His refusal to become reconciled to the New Germany that has not come to terms with the atrocities of the old Germany leads to a continuing attitude of internal exile for him. Until the arrival of Schrella, his inner emigration from the New Germany and the New Germans is characterized by a silent retreat into an abstract mode of life represented symbolically as the billiard game.

After Schrella's arrival, Robert Faehmel is able to emerge from the life of abstractions into a more active affirmation of his humanity (shown in the adoption of Hugo) and into a discontinuation of the billiard game as he had been wont to play it. Whether or not he will be able to give up his inner exile from contemporary Germany is not stated. The assumption is, however, that he cannot become reconciled to institutions that refuse to acknowledge the part they played in the past and the identity they have carved out for themselves in the present; that he cannot become reconciled to a population of conformists who lack humanity and who refuse to tolerate genuine dissenters in their midst. As long as the conditions that led to absolutism and totalitarianism persist and those in power are the people who did not oppose National Socialism but actively supported it, i.e., opportunists like Nettlinger, he cannot be reconciled.

Other surviving members of the Faehmel family who lived through totalitarianism respond similarly. On his eightieth birthday, when Heinrich Faehmel's wife demonstrates her personal courage by shooting the minister in the hope that the public action demonstrating strong opposition to the policies of the New Germany will prevent war in the future, Heinrich Faehmel is able to break with the hypocrisy—the social lie—of his life by acting publicly in accordance with the convictions he holds privately. He ceases to play the role of the social conformist, even though his break with social conventions will mean isolation and alienation from the city of Köln he loves so much. Johanna Faehmel's early exile, i.e., physical exile in the insane asylum, becomes a self-imposed inner emigration after the war when she is free to leave the mental institution but refuses to do so, chiefly because she senses in the New Germans the same ruthless, fanatical opportunism and willingness to sell out humane, civilized principles that had characterized National Socialism. When she does leave the insane asylum, it is for the express purpose of killing a former Nazi who had risen high in the new government. However, upon arriving at a parade of the New Germans with rightist leanings, she shoots a minister who, according to her opinion, would be likely to support the next war that might kill her grandson and the children of his generation. Certifiably and certified insane, she acts with impunity, knowing that she alone cannot be held responsible for this action; she knows, however, that this action will force her to continue her former inner spiritual emigration in the looney bin for life. Her act of political terrorism offered in opposition to the new government marks her willingness to continue voluntarily her exile on a permanent basis. She carries out this act—even though she realizes its futility—as a message to the New Germans, particularly those of the emerging Right, that resistance to the continuation of the old policies under totalitarianism is alive, even if only in insane asylums.

Appalled by the New Germany the returnee Schrella, too, withdraws from what he sees as a repetition of the old order parading about under the new colors of democracy. He refuses to become assimilated into this system, when Nettlinger offers to obtain financial recompensation for his suffering in exile as a political prisoner. He refuses the offer because he will not allow himself to be compromised into acquiescence with a New Germany that believes it is able to clean the black slate of the past through financial recompensation or a propaganda of reconciliation flaunted by its institutions. The lack of diversity in the New Germany is most distressing to him, particularly so because standardization and conformity to particular norms characterize not only political life, but also social, economic, and most disconcerting of all, religious life.[43] Superficial diversity is publicly displayed as evidence of a New Germany that encourages differences of opinion and life-styles, for different political parties of the right and the left are able to hold their banquets and meetings concurrently in the same hotel without even a trace of those violent political skirmishes that characterized party meetings under the Weimar Republic and the transitional years until totalitarianism eliminated all divergence; and the sheep priestess and her followers are able to follow their harmless, eccentric beliefs in full public view at the Prinz Heinrich hotel. Genuine diversity, on the other hand, is throttled even before it can possibly grow; real political dissent that might challenge the new status quo is given the death sentence through the label "communist."[44] Genuine religious challenges that threaten institutionalized religion are diffused or banished to peripheral villages, where they are rendered harmless because they are not understood by simple folk. Because real dissent is cut off by institutions to prevent it from becoming a possible challenge or alternative to the system, the nonconformist Schrella will remain in isolation; upon his return to Germany his former physical exile is replaced by a spiritual exile that is even more pronounced than that of Robert Faehmel, for it reveals an alienation from the New Germany that is deeper than that of Robert Faehmel.[44] Schrella's intellectual position in his spiritual exile constitutes the counterpart to Johanna Faehmel's radical position resulting from her internal exile in the looney bin, where she, the sane one, will be confined—possibly for life—precisely because she has preserved her sanity in a country that has adopted insane norms.

Opposing the new Germany and its *Wirtschaftswunder* in various degrees, Johanna, Robert and Heinrich Faehmel as well as Schrella have chosen permanent internal emigration. They have opted for exile in a Germany they regard as a continuation of the old, a Germany that continues to stress honor, respect, and loyalty, and a fanatical total allegiance to the government. This government stigmatizes dissenters as politically dangerous individuals whose criticism must be rendered ineffective by the pernicious label, "communist." They have chosen their inner emigration as a form of political protest against the powers that govern Germany. Is it effective? Only as long as society is aware of this exile and interprets it as an act of moral, intellectual or ideological resistance to its policies. For this reason the presence of an intellectual like Schrella is particularly important to interpret continually the meaning of this exile to a disinterested, smug, self-satisfied public that refuses to see itself in terms other than those of its self-serving, standardizing propaganda.[46] If even Ruth and Joseph Faehmel, the third generation of Faehmels, fail to comprehend the internal exile of their elders, how much more difficult must it be for society at large to understand it? Ironically enough, instead of mourning the death of Ferdi, the death of the boy who delivered messages to the Faehmels, the death of Edith and the death of victims of Nazi torture, Ruth, Joseph and Marianne visit the commercialized, cosmeticized modern German institution for programmed, controlled grieving: the Roman children's graves, where grief is evoked, channeled into a distant, impersonal antiquity, and disposed of efficiently. There New Germans can prove to themselves and the world through controlled, compassionate tears that their humanity is intact. Those who died under National Socialism in the immediate past, however, are not so remembered; and the suffering of those who went into exile—physical or spiritual—is not experienced or understood by the third generation of Faehmels. Only Hugo, Robert Faehmel's new adopted son, to whom Robert has interpreted his internal exile in countless billiard-playing sessions, understands this exile. Although Ruth, Joseph, and Marianne certainly display character traits and beliefs that may eventually force them to become dissenters, there is no guarantee that they will not become part of the materialistic, standardized life of the future.

In sum: it is evident from the novel *Billiards at Half Past Nine* that there were committed National Socialists in Germany. The novel affirms that many Nazis were inhumane people without moral fiber who continued their opportunistic stance after the war, when they simply turned colors and emerged, like the denazified Nettlinger as "democrats by conviction." It is evident that these people erased the past from their collective memories and advocated reconciliation without acknowledging their guilt or atoning for it in any way. It is true, according to the novel, that they attempted to buy off the suffering of political victims by so-called compensation or restitution. *Billiards* acknowledges that these Germans place dissent on inconsequential issues on public display so as to create the impression that the German government tolerates dissent, while in reality it stigmatizes the real dissenters with labels, such as "communist," which render the dissent ineffective.

But *Billiards at Half Past Nine* also demonstrates that there were Germans who opposed not only Hitler, but what has been called "the Hitler in us,"[47] namely those traits they observed in public conduct in Germany that might lead to the acceptance of and complicity with fascism. The novel reveals that these individuals, although in the minority, resisted oppression wherever possible and aided the oppressed as best they could. In disagreement with a repressive totalitarian government they could not openly criticize without risking death, they simultaneously expressed and concealed the form of their intellectual and ideological resistance when physical exile was not a feasible option. Their attitude can aptly be described as one of spiritual exile: in German, *innere Emigration.*

While Boell's novel confirms the appropriateness of the term, it discloses a special tragedy for those who have chosen spiritual or inner exile as their form of political opposition: those who have chosen inner emigration have done so for life. They are condemned to view the New Germany with critical detachment. While others participate enthusiastically in the formation of what they regard as a new system, they continue to live in the hotel rooms or waiting rooms of life, reflecting on the past, noting ominous parallels with the present, and fearing the future. Their inability to forget the past makes it impossible for them to give allegiance to a political system they cannot support. Their permanent exile is as much a judgment—if not a condemnation—of society as it is their personal fate. While it may be possible for someone to return from physical exile with honor, one who has chosen inner emigration will remain the outsider—will carry with him what one might call the "exile complex." Suspect in the country of which he is a citizen, he is at home in no other; reconciliation is not possible for him as it may be for some of those who have returned from physical exile. Those who have chosen permanent exile, i.e., *innere Emigration,* have in effect chosen to become the conscience of the society. Schrella is a case in point. It is his function to hold up to society continually the mirror of the past—to interpret the images of the past to a contemporary society that would prefer to ignore their significance for the past, the present, and the future.

Stressing the subjective nature of suffering in exile, Boell is careful not to weigh on the same scale the suffering of the person in spiritual exile, i.e., in inner emigration, and the suffering of the person in physical exile. One form of exile can become an extension of the other. Both entail suffering, and both are real forms of exile for those who adopt these as expressions of their opposition to political systems that do not tolerate real political dissent.

Notes

1. For a basic discussion of German literature in exile, see the essay by Hildegard Brenner, "Deutsche Literatur im Exil 1933–1947," in *Handbuch der deutschen Gegenwartsliteratur,* ed.

Hermann Kunisch (Munich: Nymphenburger Verlagshandlung, 1965), pp. 677–94. See also *Die Deutsche Exilliteratur 1933–1945*, ed. Manfred Durzak (Stuttgart: Reclam, 1973). Alexander Stephan, *Die deutsche Exilliteratur 1933–1945* (Munich: Beck, 1979). William K. Pfeiler, *German Literature in Exile,* University of Nebraska Studies n.s., 16 (Lincoln: University of Nebraska Press, 1957). Matthias Wegner, *Exil und Literatur: Deutsche Schriftsteller im Ausland. 1933–1945* (Frankfurt: Athenaeum, 1967). Helge Pross, *Die deutsche akademische Emigration nach den Vereinigten Staaten. 1933–1941* (Berlin: Duncker and Humblot, 1955). Egbert Krispyn, *Anti-Nazi Writers in Exile* (Athens: University of Georgia Press, 1978). *Exil und innere Emigration II: Internationale Tagung in St. Louis,* ed. Peter Uwe Hohendahl and Egon Schwarz, Wissenschaftliche Paperbacks Literaturwissenschaft 18 (Frankfurt: Athenaeum, 1973). *Exil und innere Emigration: Third Wisconsin Workshop,* (hereafter *Exil und innere Emigration* III), ed. Reinhold Grimm and Jost Hermand, Wissenschaftliche Paperbacks Literaturwissenschaft 17 (Frankfurt: Athenaeum, 1972).

2. Although it is difficult to assess the exodus from Germany in numbers, of the more than half a million persons who left Germany to go into exile during the reign of the National Socialists, approximately 1500 to 2500 are identified as writers. For an overview of the different groups of emigrants and their special reasons for going into exile, see Stephan, pp. 38–44. See also *Exil: literarische und politische Texte aus dem deutschen Exil 1933–1945,* ed. Ernst Loewy (Stuttgart: Metzler, 1979), pp. 465–90; Brenner, pp. 678–79, and the extensive bibliography cited there. Consult also the various volumes in Hans-Albert Walter's monumental work, *Deutsche Exilliteratur 1933–1950* 1, 2, 7 (Darmstadt: Luchterhand, 1972, 1974); 4 (Stuttgart: Metzler, 1978).

3. Manfred Durzak, "Literarische Diaspora. Stationen des Exils," in *Die deutsche Exilliteratur 1933–1945,* ed. Manfred Durzak, pp. 40–55. Conditions of exile in various countries are discussed in this work, pp. 56–182. See also Krispyn, *Anti-Nazi Writers,* chap. 6, pp. 59–85. For personal accounts by emigrants, see *Verbannung: Aufzeichnungen deutscher Schriftsteller im Exil,* ed. Egon Schwarz and Matthias Wegner (Hamburg: Christian Wegner Verlag, 1964), pp. 63–160. Cf. also Wegner, *Exil und Literatur,* as well as Loewy, *Exil,* pp. 491–557.

4. The Emergency Rescue Committee, a private body founded by American authors, helped thousands to escape to the United States, in spite of these restrictions. For a discussion of United States immigration restrictions, see Krispyn, *Anti-Nazi Writers,* pp. 105–121, as well as Arthur D. Morse, *While Six Million Died: A Chronicle of American Apathy* (New York: Ace Publishing Corporation, n. d.).

5. A poignant portrayal of the difficulties of living in exile emerges from the various accounts found in *Verbannung,* pp. 57–160. See also, Egon Krispyn, "Exil als Lebensform," in *Exil und innere Emigration II,* pp. 100–18. Hans Mayer, "Konfrontation der inneren und der äusseren Emigration: Erinnerung und Deutung," in *Exil und innere Emigration* III, pp. 75–88. Wegner, *Exil und Literatur,* pp. 86–110.

6. *Exil* (Amsterdam: Querido, 1940), p. 151. In spite of sharp differences among them, writers in exile enjoyed a greater degree of cohesiveness than did any other group. See Klaus Mann, "Rechenschaft," in *Verbannung,* pp. 280–81. Also Hans Mayer, "Konfrontation." Jost Hermand, "Schreiben in der Fremde. Gedanken zur deutschen Exilliteratur seit 1789," in *Exil und innere Emigration* III, offers a perceptive grouping of writers in exile. (See pp. 16–30.)

7. Herbert Lehnert, "Repräsentation und Zweifel. Thomas Manns Exilwerke und der deutsche Kulturbürger," in Durzak, *Die deutsche Exilliteratur 1933–1945,* pp. 398–417. Important address, speeches, and essays of Thomas Mann during his exile are found in Loewy, *Exil.* See also Wegner, pp. 111–130, and the works listed above in note 1. Bertolt Brecht, as is well known, emerged as another major spokesman of writers in exile, particularly those on the Left. See Ulrich Weisstein, "Bertold Brecht. Die Lehren des Exils," in Durzak, *Die deutsche Exilliteratur 1933–1945,* pp. 373–97. Other important spokespersons are also accorded separate treatment in Durzak's collection.

8. Hans Mayer, pp. 75–88. Grimm, "Innere Emigration als Lebensform," *Exil und innere Emigration* III, p. 41. Wolfgang Brekle, "Die antifaschistische Literatur in Deutschland (1933–1945)," *Weimarer Beiträge* 16 (1970): 67–69.

9. Brekle, pp. 68–128. Herbert Wiesner, "'Innere Emigration' Die innerdeutsche Literatur im Widerstand 1933–1945," in *Handbuch der deutschen Gegenwartsliteratur,* ed. Hermann Kunisch, pp. 695–720. H. R. Klieneberger, *The Christian Writers of the Inner Emigration,* Anglica

Germanica British Studies in Germanic Languages and Literatures, 10 (The Hague: Mouton, 1968). Charles Hoffmann, *Opposition Poetry in Nazi Germany* (Berkeley: University of California Press, 1962). Many more perspectives could be cited.

10. Ernst Barlach and Ricarda Huch are cases in point. For discussions of these and others who were part of the resistance to National Socialism, see Brekle, pp. 101–6. See also Günther Weisenborn, ed., *Der lautlose Aufstand. Bericht über die Widerstandsbewegung des deutschen Volkes*, 1933–45 (Hamburg: Rowohlt 1953). Materials for this book were provided by Ricarda Huch and Walter Hammer.

11. For a history of the term and a rather objective discussion of the controversy surrounding it, see Brekle, p. 70. While some, such as F. Schonauer and H. Baumgart, are opposed to the use of the term altogether, documented opposition to National Socialism within Germany of those who claimed intellectual, moral, and ideological alienation from totalitarianism suggests that the term is appropriate as a description of this attitude. Brekle and Hoffmann concur; however, both carefully limit its use to a descriptive term.

12. For a discussion of literature produced by writers to whom one may attribute inner emigration, see Hoffman, *Opposition Poetry in Nazi Germany*, pp. 133 ff. See also Klieneberger, *The Christian Writers of the Inner Emigration*, for a portrayal of Christian writers of inner emigration, whose opposition to National Socialism was based on Christian precepts.

13. In this vein writes Ernst Loewy, "Der Anti-Nazi war für das KZ designiert, sofern er nicht das Exil vorzog" ("Whoever opposed national socialism was marked for concentration camp, unless he preferred exile"). *Literatur unterm Hakenkreuz: Das Dritte Reich und seine Dichtung*, Fischer Bücherei 1042 (Frankfurt, 1969), p. 270.

It is estimated that about 300,000 German opponents of National Socialism died in concentration camps and that another 200,000 were incarcerated but survived the ordeal. Jost Hermand, "Schreiben in der Fremde," *Exil und innere Emigration* III, p. 29.

14. Sharply divergent views on the question of a possible return to Germany are found in *Verbannung*, "Ausblick", pp. 269–309. Alfred Polgar summarizes the problematical confrontation between those who had stayed in Germany and those who returned from exile as follows: "Die zufällig nicht umgebracht wurden, müssen ihren Frieden machen mit denen, die zufällig nicht mehr dazu gekommen sind, sie umzubringen." ("Those who by chance were not killed have to come to terms with those who accidentally didn't get around to killing them") (*Verbannung*, p. 277). See also Krispyn, *Anti-Nazi Writers*, chap. 10 and Hans Mayer, "Konfrontation," pp. 83–87.

15. For Frank Thiess's letter and the correspondence surrounding the issue of Thomas Mann's return, see *Die grosse Kontroverse: Ein Briefwechsel um Deutschland*, ed. J. F. G. Grosser (Hamburg: Nagel Verlag, 1963). See also Polgar, "Innere und äussere Emigration," *Verbannung*, 276–78.

16. See Walter von Molo's open letter to Thomas Mann of 4 August 1945, published in the *Münchner Zeitung* on 13 August 1945 in *Die grosse Kontroverse*, pp. 18–21. "Kommen Sie bald wie ein guter Arzt, der nicht nur die Wirkung sieht, sondern die Ursache der Krankheit sucht und diese vornehmlich zu beheben bemüht ist, der allerdings auch weiss, dass chirurgische Eingriffe nötig sind, vor allem bei den zahlreichen, die einmal Wert darauf gelegt haben, geistig genannt zu werden. . . ." ("Come to us like a good physician, who observes not only the effect of the disease, but searches for its cause and whose first concern it is to remove the cause of the disease; be the physician who recognizes also, however, that surgery is necessary, especially among the many, to whom it was once important to be called intellectuals") (p. 20).

17. See Frank Thiess, "Die innere Emigration," in *Die grosse Kontroverse*, pp. 22–25, and Thomas Mann's reply, published in the *Augsburger Anzeiger* of 12 October 1945, "Warum ich nicht zurückkehre," in *Die grosse Kontroverse*, pp. 27–36.

18. Others, such as E. Glaeser, who had returned to Germany from abroad to live under the rule of National Socialism and who had occupied a relatively high position that required the trust of the government, claimed to have returned courageously to Germany to share its fate. Krispyn, *Anti-Nazi Writers*, p. 102.

19. *Die grosse Kontroverse*, p. 13: Es mag Aberglaube sein, aber in meinen Augen sind Bücher, die von 1933 bis 1945 in Deutschland überhaupt gedruckt werden konnten, weniger als wertlos und nicht gut in die Hand zu nehmen. Ein Geruch von Blut und Schande haftet ihnen an. Sie sollten alle eingestampft werden. ("It may be nothing more than superstition, but

books, which could be printed in Germany from 1933 to 1945, are absolutely worthless and should not be taken into one's hands. An odor of blood and shame clings to them. They should all be reduced to pulp").

20. Schonauer, *Deutsche Literatur im Dritten Reich,* p. 125 ff. Emil Ludwig, "Was soll mit Deutschland geschehen?" *Aufbau* 8, no. 30 (1942). Thomas Mann, in an address delivered in the Coolidge Auditorium in the Library of Congress on the evening of 20 May 1945, affirmed,

> . . . there are not two Germanys, a good one and a bad one, but only one, whose best turned into evil through devilish cunning. Wicked Germany is merely good Germany gone astray, good Germany in misfortune, in guilt, and ruin. (*Thomas Mann's Addresses Delivered at the Library of Congress 1942–1949* [Washington: Library of Congress, 1963], p. 64).

21. Whether or not Germany should be considered collectively guilty for atrocities committed under National Socialism was debated heatedly by those in exile. See *Verbannung,* "Ausblick," pp. 269–309. For those, who believed in collective guilt, see above note 20. Writers of the Left, such as Bertolt Brecht, Alfred Kantorowics ("Der deutsche Geist in der Diaspora," *Moderne Sprak* 62 [1968]: 282), and Hanna Arendt opposed the placement of collective guilt on all Germans who had remained in Germany between 1933 and 1945. See Jost Hermand, "Schreiben in der Fremde," in *Exil und innere Emigration* III, p. 25.

22. Joseph Wulf, *Literatur und Dichtung im Dritten Reich: Eine Dokumentation* (Gütersloh: Mohn, 1963); and Dietrich Strothmann, *Nationalsozialistische Literaturpolitik: Ein Beitrag zur Publizistik im Dritten Reich,* 2d ed. (Bonn: Bouvier, 1963). Cf. note 2, above.

23. *Die deutsche Literatur der Gegenwart* (München: Nymphenburger Verlag, 1957), p. 15:

> Man spricht von einer Literatur der "inneren Emigranten", im Gegensatz zu jener Literatur, die von Emigranten ausserhalb Deutschlands geschrieben wurde. Die Bezeichnung ist insofern nicht glücklich, als "innere Emigration" überhaupt der Weg war, den das Dritte Reich die Literatur zu gehen zwang. . . . Dem Schriftsteller wurde auf jede Weise nahe gelegt, seinen Rückzug aus der Öffentlichkeit anzutreten. . . . Insofern können wir von "innerer Emigration" auch bei Staatsschriftstellern des Dritten Reiches sprechen. Die Emigration in die Historie, die Kolbenheyer, Walter von Molo, Friedrich Blunck und Wilhelm Schäfer bereits vor 1933 angetreten hatten, wurde zur Heerstrasse schwächerer Schriftsteller. (One speaks of a literature of the "internal exile movement" in opposition to that literature, that was written by emigrants outside of Germany. The designation is not felicitious in as much as "internal exile" was the path which literature was forced to take by the Third Reich. . . . The writer was admonished in every possible way to embark on his withdrawal from public life. . . . For that reason one can refer to "internal exile" even in connection with writers officially recognized by the Third Reich. Emigration into history, upon which Kolbenheyer, Walter von Molo, Friedrich Blunck, and Wilhelm Schaefer had already embarked before 1933, became became the route for the flood of less able writers").

24. The significance of such a reception by readers similarly opposed to fascism is discussed by Hoffman, "Opposition und innere Emigration," *Exil und innere Emigration* II, p. 134 ff. For the readership of journals that printed oppositional literature, see Hans-Albert Walter, *Exilpresse 1, Deutsche Exilliteratur 1933–1950,* no. 7 (Darmstadt: Luchterhand, 1974).

25. Walter A. Berendsohn, "Innere Emigration," (position paper, 1971), p. 4. Schonauer, *Deutsche Literatur im Dritten Reich,* p. 148. Charles Hoffmann, "Opposition und innere Emigration," provides a useful delineation of positions on the use of the term "innere Emigration."

26. Hoffmann, "Opposition und innere Emigration," p. 131, but see his larger discussion of the term, pp. 128–132. Wiesner, "Innere Emigration," in Kunisch, *Handbuch,* p. 698, limits the use of the term to that literature, "deren Grundhaltung vom geistigen Widerstand gegen die Herrschaft des 'Dritten Reiches' bestimmt war. . . . Wir haben darunter eine untrennbare Verbindung von Oppositionsgeist und einer der personalen Emigration vergleichbaren, absichtlichen oder erzwungenen Distanzierung von der national-sozialistischen Herrschaft zu verstehen" ("whose basic position was determined by spiritual opposition to the government of the Third Reich. . . . By this we understand an inseparable link between a spirit of opposition to National Socialism and an intentional separation from it achieved through great exertion, which can be compared to personal exile"). Cf. also Brekle, "Antifaschistische

Literatur," p. 71. "Zur Literatur der inneren Emigration wird die Literatur gezählt, deren Autoren wie die Schriftsteller des Exils von der Nazi-Ideologie nicht beeinflusst waren, humanistische Werke schrieben und sich von der faschistischen Politik nicht gleichschalten liessen. Unter innerdeutscher antifaschistischer Literatur wird nur der Teil dieser Literatur verstanden, der als Mittel des antifaschistischen Widerstandes oder als Ausdruck anti-faschistischer Haltung zwischen 1933 und 1945 in Deutschland geschrieben wurde" ("As part of the literature of internal exile we count that literature whose authors, like the authors of the exile movement, were not influenced by Nazi ideology, who wrote humanistic books and refused to be brought into line by fascist politics. By German anti-fascist literature we understand only that special part of this literature, which was written in Germany between 1933 and 1945 as a means of offering opposition to fascism or as an expression of a basic opposition to fascism").

27. Hoffman, "Opposition und innere Emigration," p. 131.

28. Hans Mayer, p. 83. See also notes 14 and 16, above. Cf. also chapter 6 of Heinrich Böll's novel *Billiard um halb zehn* (1959) in Heinrich Böll, *Werke, Romane und Erzählungen* 3, 1954–1959, ed. Bernd Balzer (Cologne: Kiepenheuer & Witsch, 1977), pp. 292–535.

29. See note 23.

30. Quotations in the text will be made from the English translation of the book by Leila Vennewitz, *Billiards at Half Past Nine* (New York: Avon, Bard Books, 1975). In the footnotes the German text will accompany the English translation to allow the reader to compare the two.

31. See *Billiards at Half Past Nine,* especially chap. 4, e.g.,

From the moment I set foot in the city I had my moves all figured out, an exact daily routine, the steps of a complicated dance all down to a tee—myself soloist and ballet master all in one. Cast and decor were there for the asking, not costing a penny. (p. 67).

But now the myth I had it in mind to propagate was about to take shape. Indeed, it was already on the way toward its goal when the cook's "Paprika cheese?" echoed my order. What was this goal? The Public. (p. 76)

But see also pp. 77–82, 84, 94, 105, 110, and elsewhere.

32. *Billiards at Half Past Nine,* p. 88 and elsewhere.

33. *Billiards at Half Past Nine,* p. 99.

34. *Billiards at Half Past Nine,* pp. 110, 137–38, and elsewhere.

35. *Billiard um halb zehn:* Johanna sprach aus, was ich dachte; (363)

. . . und [ich] sagte nicht, was ich hätte sagen müssen, dass ich ihr zustimmte, ich sagte: "Schwanger, meine Herren, . . ." und wusste doch, dass ich hätte sagen müssen: ich stimme meiner Frau zu; wusste, dass Ironie nicht ausreichte und nie ausreichen würde. (pp. 363–64)

36. *Billiard um halb zehn:*

". . . und ich weiss, dass es eine Möglichkeit gab, den Mördern zu entrinnen: für verrückt erklärt zu werden;" (p. 421)
". . . still, Alter, weine doch nicht, ich lebte in der inneren Emigration. . . ." (p. 422)

37. *Billiard um halb zehn:*

"Ich werde nicht zur Einweihung kommen," dachte Robert, "weil ich nicht versöhnt bin, nicht versöhnt mit den Kräften, die Ferdis Tod verschuldeten, und nicht mit denen, die Ediths Tod verschuldeten und Sankt Severin schonten; ich bin nicht versöhnt, nicht versöhnt mit mir und nicht mit dem Geist der Versöhnung, den Sie bei Ihrer Festansprache verkünden werden; es war nicht blinder Eifer, der Ihre Heimstatt zerstörte, sondern Hass, der nicht blind war und dem noch keine Reue erwachsen ist. Soll ich bekennen, dass ich es gewesen bin? Ich muss meinem Vater Schmerz zufügen, obwohl er nicht schuldig ist, und vielleicht meinem Sohn, obwohl auch er nicht schuldig ist, und Ihnen, Ehrwürdiger Vater, obwohl auch Sie nicht schuldig sind; wer ist schon schuldig? Ich bin nicht versöhnt mit der Welt, in der eine Handbewegung und ein missverstandenes Wort das Leben kostet." Und er sagte: "Herzlichen Dank, Ehrwürdiger Vater, es wird mir eine Freude sein, an Ihrem Fest teilzunehmen." (p. 489)

38. *Billiard um halb zehn:*

Sie waren alle dazu verdammt, vom *Sakrament des Büffels* zu kosten, wie meine Brüder; jung waren sie nur an Jahren, und es gab für sie alle nur eins, das ihnen Glanz versprach, ihnen Grösse verleihen, sie in mythischen Dunst hüllen würde: den Tod; Zeit war nur ein Mittel, sie ihm entgegen zu tragen; sie schnupperten danach, und alles, was danach roch, war ihnen gut; sie rochen selbst danach: Verwesung; sie hockte im Haus, in den Augen derer, denen ich vorgeworfen werden sollte: Mützenträger, Gesetzeshüter; nur eins war verboten: leben wollen und spielen. Verstehst du mich, Alter? Spiel galt als Todsünde; nicht Sport, den hätten sie geduldet; das hält lebendig, macht anmutig, hübsch, steigert den Appetit der Wölfe; Puppenstuben: gut; das fördert die hausfraulichen und mütterlichen Instinkte: tanzen: auch gut; das gehört zum Markt; aber wenn ich für mich ganz allein tanzte, im Hemd oben in meinem Zimmer: Sünde, weil es nicht Pflicht war; . . . . ich betete um den, der mich erretten, vom Tode im Wolfszwinger erlösen würde, ich betete und nahm das weisse *Sakrament* drauf und sah dich im Atelierfenster drüben. (p. 420)

39. *Billiards at Half Past Nine,* pp. 171, 248.
40. *Billiard um halb zehn:*

[Schrella to Nettlinger]
"Es würde mir leid tun," sagte Schrella, "wenn du glaubtest, dass ich die Echtheit deiner Motive und Gefühle bezweifle. Nicht einmal deine Reue ziehe ich in Zweifel, aber Bilder— und du hast mich gebeten, die Geschichte als Bild in meine Sammlung aufzunehmen—, Bilder bedeuten eine Abstraktion, und das ist die Rolle, die du damals gespielt hast und heute spielst; die Rollen sind—verzeih—die gleichen, denn damals bedeutete mich unschädlich zu machen, mich einzusperren, heute bedeutet mich unschädlich zu machen, mich freizulassen; ich fürchte, dass Robert, der viel abstrakter denkt als ich, aus diesem Grund keinen Wert darauf legt, dich zu treffen." (p. 443)

41. *Billiards at Half Past Nine,* pp. 36, 50, 61, and elsewhere.
42. *Billiards at Half Past Nine,* pp. 244–45, 248.
43. *Billiards at Half Past Nine,* pp. 246, 247, 248.
44. *Billiards at Half Past Nine,* p. 248.
45. *Billiards at Half Past Nine,* pp. 246–47.
46. *Billiards at Half Past Nine,* pp. 163, 245–47.
47. E.g., Max Picard, *Hitler in uns selbst* (Zurich: Eugen Rentsch Verlag, 1946). Thomas Mann frequently referred to "Bruder Hitler." See his essay, "Bruder Hitler," in *Reden und Aufsätze,* Gesammelte Werke 12 (Oldenburg: Fischer, 1960), pp. 845–52.

Testimonies from Exile: Works by Hernán Valdés, Eduardo Galeano, and David Viñas

MARIA-INES LAGOS-POPE

Exile is not a new condition in Spanish American letters.[1] On the contrary, taken in a broad sense, it has been an experience common to a large number of writers and intellectuals throughout history. In the nineteenth century some of the foremost examples are those of Bello, Montalvo, Hostos, Martí, Sarmiento, and the group of Argentinian exiles in Chile and Uruguay, and in the twentieth century Vallejo, Neruda, and Alfonso Reyes. More recently those in the foreground are Cabrera Infante, Roa Bastos, and Onetti, to mention only a few. It is not surprising, then, that many important works have been written in exile. *Facundo,* one of the highlights of nineteenth century Spanish American literature, was written in and shaped by exile and is an example of how literature can be used as a political weapon.[2]

In *Ensayos sobre subversión,* H. A. Murena bemoans the fact that throughout its history Latin American literature has been linked to politics.[3] He writes that with the exception of works in which the artistic and aesthetic qualities have surpassed the historical circumstances in which they originated—he mentions *Facundo* as an example—this has given the literature an ephemeral character. On the other hand, Murena explains that many works, like Montalvo's essays, have lost their acclaim, as they were written with the primary intention of attacking the then current regimes. Thus, when Montalvo's political enemy the dictator García Moreno died, Montalvo could write his now famous sentence: "My pen killed him."

It is this connection between literature and politics that I would like to explore in three works written in exile, which are directly linked to the political events that have taken place in the Southern Cone nations in the last decade. Yet although they were inspired by these events and refer to them, they are highly literary creations. This can be seen in their use of language,

121

structure, and genre. By means of aesthetic distance they have surpassed the political and historical circumstances in which they originated.[4]

The three works that I have selected to exemplify this situation are: *Tejas Verdes* (*Diario de un campo de concentración en Chile*) (1974), by the Chilean Hernán Valdés; *Días y noches de amor y de guerra* (1978), by Eduardo Galeano, from Uruguay; and *Cuerpo a cuerpo* (1979), by David Viñas, from Argentina. These authors are well-known and established writers who have suffered political exile in a strict sense. Since I will be using the term exile frequently throughout this study it seems appropriate at this point to specify more concretely what I mean by exile. I will follow the definition that Paul Tabori has put forth in *The Anatomy of Exile:* "An exile is a person compelled to leave or remain outside his country of origin on account of well-founded fear of persecution for reasons of race, religion, nationality, or political opinion; a person who considers his exile temporary (even though it may last a lifetime), hoping to return to his fatherland when circumstances permit, but unable to do so as long as the factors that made him an exile persist."[5]

Prior to an analysis of these texts, I would like to point out some aspects that they have in common. First, these works do not address exile itself, but rather exemplify a type of narrative written in exile. In "The Writer in Exile or the Literature of Exile and Counter-Exile," Claudio Guillén distinguishes between two types of narratives of exile. In the first, "exile becomes its own subject matter," and it often belongs to the elegiac mode. In the second, "exile is the condition but not the visible cause of an imaginative response often characterized by a tendency toward integration, increasingly broad vistas or universalism." He calls this literature of counter-exile.[6] The three narratives that I am addressing belong to the second kind. Exceptions to this are sections of Galeano's *Días y noches,* when the narrator nostalgically recalls his life in Uruguay from his exile in Buenos Aires or remembers the camaraderie with friends of his past from his exile in Spain. In other words, exile has made it possible for these works to have been written and published, and more importantly, to be publicized, distributed, and read.

It is no coincidence that these three authors were in exile in Spain. This is true not only because the cultural and linguistic similarities between Spain and their native countries made Spain a comfortable and convenient alternative but because Spain has traditionally been a haven for intellectuals escaping Latin American dictatorial regimes. This may seem contradictory, and it is, to a certain extent, for until 1975 Spain was ruled by the Fascist *caudillo* Francisco Franco. One should remember, however, that Spain has been the traditional sanctuary for both right- and left-wing exiles, even in the Franco years. In the 1960s, moreover, many novels that severely criticized the Latin American military were published there. One example is *La ciudad y los perros* (1962) by Mario Vargas Llosa, which provoked a scandal in

Perú. It is important to remember that the publishing industry is, after tourism, one of the major sources of hard currency for Spain. In order to illustrate the extent to which economic factors determine that which is published or banished, censored or allowed, I will refer briefly to the circumstances under which *Tejas Verdes* was published.

As with any other work published in Spain, *Tejas Verdes,* was submitted to the censorship of the Ministry of Information and Tourism. The censors decided that Valdés's narrative was a complete hoax and advised that it not be published. The editor, however, risking the confiscation of the entire edition, went ahead and published the diary.[7] By a stroke of luck and *franquista* vengeance the publication was distributed freely. The Chilean Military Junta cancelled a commercial transaction signed during the Allende years, and instead of buying trucks from Spain they acquired them in the United States. In retaliation, the Spanish Government authorized the publication of *Tejas Verdes.* This incident demonstrates the ways in which economic factors exert a decisive pressure in cultural matters. It is interesting to note that Valdés's diary was a great success among the reading public. It was immediately translated into English, Swedish, Dutch, Danish, Norwegian, German, Portugese, Hungarian, and Italian.[8]

A second feature that these works share is their direct relation to the historical, social and political conditions that encouraged their authors' exile. These conditions are fully described in each of the narratives. In this sense they are literary responses to the political repression exerted by the military regimes of Chile, Argentina, and Uruguay.

A third common thread in these works is the fact that they involve a journalist or writer who gives testimony of true or fictitious experiences that ultimately pushed him to exile. It is a fact that after politicians and union leaders, intellectuals have been among the most persecuted groups in these countries because of their capacity to express their horrific experiences and instigate subversion or reflection with their writings. Thus exile, with its aftermath of persecution, forced estrangement from the native land, and violence as a traumatic experience, shapes these works in different ways. It provides their authors with the necessary distance to reflect upon the circumstances that lead them into banishment.

However, in spite of the fact that these narratives show the imprint of historical events, and, at least in the case of *Tejas Verdes,* have an immediate informative role, they do not cease to be autonomous and complete. This is clearly exemplified in Valdés's case. In the prologue to the 1978 edition of his book he had to modify his statement of 1974 in which he maintained that his diary "was written with the intention of producing an immediate reaction in the reader, to incite him to rebellion, to stir up his solidarity with respect to concrete facts, before new statistics with the same attributes but applied to a different subject appeared in the papers" (7).[9] Nevertheless, after the success of his book Valdés declared that his diary was no longer an instrument of immediate denunciation, but rather, as he wants it to be, a permanent instrument of denunciation (cf. 9).

In an essay entitled "Defensa de la palabra," Eduardo Galeano writes that "to maintain that literature by itself is going to change reality would be an act of madness or of arrogance," although he thinks that it can certainly help.[10] The purpose of these narratives is to give testimony, since "by writing it is possible to offer, in spite of persecution and censorship, testimonies of our time and our people," and to tell what memory can preserve before it succumbs to oblivion.[11] These three works have originated from a process of crisis and change, and they are firmly rooted, borrowing Galeano's words, in the risks and adventures of their times. One of their aims is to help create, as he puts it, symbols of the new reality by shedding light on the "signs" of the road.[12] The relationship with the historical events is not avoided; on the contrary, it is stressed.

In order to approach these narratives from a literary perspective and delineate more precisely their relationship with the historical events that inspired them, it is necessary to consider them from the point of view of the genre to which they belong. This is possible because all of them correspond to very distinct genres, which have been clearly defined by literary tradition.[13]

The first of these, *Tejas Verdes,* is a reconstructed diary that recounts the series of events that befell the author from the moment he arrived home on the evening of 12 February 1974 until the time when he was freed, on 15 March of the same year. These events include the search of his house and his detention by police. The difference between this diary written *a posteriori* and a conventional diary written day by day lies in the fact that the author has been able to carefully select his material. He writes from the perspective of someone who knows the outcome of his adventure, or misadventure; he transcribes what is relevant and avoids futile details or repetitions. This focus allows him to incorporate *post facto* reflections that create distance between the present in which he writes and the present of the narration. We find an example of this distanced view in the following passage: "He doesn't say anything, but there is a strange silence that, at that moment, I was not able to understand" (123). In a diary such as Valdés's, narrator and author are one, a fact that provides not only unity, but adds testimonial value to the text.

Valdés's diary starts by describing the destruction, slow disintegration, and change that is occurring in his world. The narrator writes: "There are fewer and fewer recognizable faces left in the city" (12). Many of his acquaintances are leaving the country for fear of persecution, torture, and death. Personal relationships are being broken and substituted for transitory, precarious ones. Even before being apprehended by the police, the need to leave becomes apparent to the narrator, especially when he remembers that "three days ago Eva left home," "yesterday Sara departed for Buenos Aires." He decides to leave for "wherever he can" (11).

From the first lines of the diary there is an emphasis on the incoherence of the situation the narrator is going through: "What exactly am I doing here, at home, at 6:30 in the evening? I could not explain it to anyone in a coherent way" (11). Although the insecurity and instability in which he lives are constantly emphasized, the narrator has not yet lost confidence in rationality and common sense. When the police apprehend him he is not especially worried, as his most compromising articles seem not to have been discovered. He thinks: "I am sure that a statement before a reasonable person will clear things up and that I will be able to be back in a short while. It doesn't even occur to me to put on a jacket or change my sandals for shoes" (18). It does not take long, however, for his confidence to disappear. The arbitrary and brutal methods of his torturers soon teach him that proving his innocence or telling the truth is beside the point. He is not informed of where he will be taken, nor is he outrightly accused; instead he is submitted to physical and psychological torture (mistreatment, humiliation, degradation, hunger, cold, and violence). Such treatment leaves him feeling guilty, cowardly, and frightened.

The prisoner's world is governed by a strict order and routine that make no apparent sense. For instance, he must awaken at dawn and go out for a few minutes, only to return to his cabin to do nothing for the rest of the day. Having all day to meditate on his situation, his uncertainty increases. He tries to guess what is going on outside, what will happen, when he will be interrogated, and so on. None of the prisoners know why they have been detained. This uncertainty is reflected in such grammatical forms as "it must have finished," "perhaps," "anything could happen. They are free to do with us what they wish" (53).

The defenselessness of the prisoners is augmented by the power of the guards and the military officers. In addition, life in the city continues as usual, as if nothing had happened. The city "pretends to continue living in complete innocence" (51). This routine leads to the weakening of the will and the defenses, and to the total destruction of the individual, who becomes passive and agrees to sign false statements that distort his confessions. He does this because he realizes that his only hope of getting out alive is to admit his guilt. Finally the narrator comes to the conclusion that his detention "is a situation in itself. Somewhere there is a rationale that has determined it and whose intentions, like God's, are inscrutable" (35).

The procedures employed by the authorities to transform and reeducate the prisoners in order to make them harmless and absolutely passive are by no means new or peculiar to certain regimes. In his historical works, Michel Foucault has shown how power is exercised in the different realms of society. He says that by using the discipline of the penal system as a method or strategy, society has shaped the modern individual. This strategy has been used not only in the army and in prisons, but also in schools, clinics, and factories. "We are in the society of the teacher-judge, the education-judge, the 'social-worker'-judge; it is on them that the universal reign of the normative is based; and each individual, wherever he may find himself, subjects his body, his gestures, his behavior, his aptitudes, his achievements. The carceral network, in its compact or disseminated forms, with its systems of insertion, distribution, surveillance, observation, has been the greatest support, in modern society, of the normalizing power."[14] According-ing to Foucault's analysis it is the carceral methods of society that have "objectified human behaviour," which are at the root of the mechanisms and strategies of power.[15]

Thus, the discovery that the narrator of *Tejas Verdes* makes through experience corresponds to a strategy of power that has been developed and refined in the last two centuries and whose rationale has been examined by Foucault in *Discipline and Punish*. As can be seen in *Tejas Verdes,* especially in the accounts of other prisoners that Valdés includes in his diary, "torture is a technique; it is not an extreme expression of lawless rage."[16] One could postulate, moreover, that torture, like public execution in the seventeenth and eighteenth centuries, "is to be understood not only as a judicial, but also as a political ritual. It belongs, even in minor cases, to the ceremonies by which power is manifested."[17]

In many ways the activities of the concentration camp parallel the public execution ceremonies of older days. For this reason I will quote some of the functions and purposes Foucault attributes to them.

> The public execution, however hasty and everyday, belongs to a whole series of great rituals in which power is eclipsed and restored (coronation, entry of the king into a conquered city, the submission of rebellious subjects); over and above the crime that has placed the sovereign in contempt, it deploys before all eyes an invincible force. Its aim is not so much to re-establish a balance as to bring into play, as its extreme point, the dissymmetry between the subject who has dared to violate the law and the all-powerful sovereign who displays his strength. . . . The public execution did not re-establish justice; it reactivated power. . . . Its ruthlessness, its spectacle, its physical violence, its unbalanced play of forces, its meticulous ceremonial, its entire apparatus were inscribed in the political functioning of the penal system.[18]

In short, Foucault has shown the historical development of the punishment tactics and the rationale behind them. Nothing is left to chance; there is only the discipline of punishment. This is precisely what is demonstrated by literary means in these three works.

Tejas Verdes not only describes the horror, brutality, and apparent irrationality of repression, but also reflects on some of the mistakes of Popular Unity, the political coalition that brought Salvador Allende into power in 1970. Special emphasis is placed on the workers' lack of information with respect to the strength and organization of the opposition. The diary also mentions the dilemma of a Left, lead by men who belonged to the *bourgeoisie* or *petite bourgeoisie*. The labeling of all opposing forces with the term "fascist" in a premature and importune gesture is criticized because it contributed to the obstruction of the term's meaning and prevented an impartial analysis of the metamorphosis of the right-wing parties. Valdés also mentions the "tourists of the revolution who have come from a world where revolution is allowed only as an object of intellectual consumption" (86), an allusion to sympathizers from the developed world who went to Chile to witness the socialist revolution.

The author does not directly denounce any of his captors, not even the United States. The United States is mentioned on two or three occasions to indicate that on this or that object one can read "U.S. Army," as on the showers of the concentration camp.[19] Nevertheless, Valdés condemns the attitude of the poet Nicanor Parra, who called himself a socialist when Allende was in power but later briefly collaborated with the military junta. The author also criticizes class prejudices, an attitude condoned by the military, through a description of one of the prisoners who almost won a race in the Berlin Olympics of 1936 but was prevented from winning by malicious methods.

Just by recording the horrors of torture, the cruel methods, and the lack of compassion and humanity, *Tejas Verdes* denounces the brutality of the military system. The diary has preserved the freshness and spontaneity of the testimony, and it is this that captures and moves the reader.

The second work, *Días y noches de amor y de guerra,* by the Uruguayan Eduardo Galeano, was the winner in 1978 of the prestigious *Casa de las Américas* Award. In an interview with the Spanish newspaper *El País* the author asserted that his book "is like a report to one's own memory. All that is told there took place."[20] In this narrative Galeano recalls episodes of his childhood in Uruguay, his travels and friendships, his love affairs, and his work as director of the journal *Crisis* in Buenos Aires from 1975 until the closing of the publication in 1976, when he went into exile in Spain.

In *Días y noches* the narrative discourse is structured around a fairly precise temporal sequence that corresponds to the period when Galeano was an exile in Buenos Aires and worked for *Crisis.* Although the narrative is told in the first person, it is not a diary, but rather a memoir.[21] In the memoir the center of attraction is not the person of the author in itself, but the events in which he participates or that he witnesses. His authority lies in the fact that he witnessed certain events. And as he participated in these experiences or heard them from other witnesses, his role is to serve as a unifying element to the discourse.

Días y noches is a narrative made up of fragments: memories, auto-biographical episodes, news, and stories that the narrator has been gathering and compiling in his memory throughout his pilgrimage to different lands of America. The witness-narrator, whose role is to preserve the past through writing, gives cohesiveness to the discourse.

From the chaos that seems to pervade his memoirs, certain constant features emerge and provide a coherent structure for the narrative. Among these constant features are the autobiographical episodes that evoke child-hood experiences, adolescence, love affairs, travels, and other important aspects of his life. There are also three installment-type series inserted at different points in the narrative. The first is called "The Universe as Seen through a Keyhole," where magical and marvelous stories related to child-hood are told. The second is "News," and the third, "The System," which appears fourteen times. The latter describes the system of destruction and extermination that dominates and subjugates the individual. Here Galeano describes the fight for power, the economic war, and the class struggle. By explaining the causes of the "Goodbyes"—the terror, disappearances, and persecution—this series sheds light on incidents experienced by different individuals. Galeano shows how the machine teaches acceptance of horror as something natural, how censorship turns one's own house into a jail, how it destroys solidarity through forced denunciations, how it exercises vio-lence without shooting (economic violence), and how it seeks to extermi-nate everything alive, even grass, and especially memory. In short, it destroys life because it is "sterile, and hates everything that grows and moves."[22]

The author points out that this is a calculated war, not an isolated occurrence, because he has seen the same thing happening in other places: Argentina in 1956–57, Guatemala in 1967, Argentina in 1977, and so on. The sad, ironic thing is that while Latin American scientists must emigrate, the wielders of power "contribute to advances in methods of torture, techniques for assassinating people and ideas, the cultivation of silence, the multiplication of powerlessness and the spreading of fear" (159).

Another element that helps to structure the narrative is memory. Because he has a conscience capable of knowing and a memory capable of remem-bering, the narrator is able to give testimony of what he has witnessed. His task is especially significant, as Galeano points out in an essay, because "our collective identity stems from the past and is nurtured by it."[23] For this reason it becomes necessary to transmit these stories to future generations. A living example of this preoccupation is Eric, who desires that his newborn child "not be able to believe that all of this was once possible" (80). But first it must be written in the annals of history.

Thus remembrance, memory, becomes a challenge to the exterminating plans of the system that forbids the act of remembering. The narrator recalls a time when "things were discussed out loud, when one could walk in the streets without identification papers; no one was afraid" (142), and this, he suggests, cannot be forgotten.

Another device that gives coherence to the narration are the "Goodbyes." *Días y noches* starts by recalling a story that was told to the narrator in Caracas. When Edda Armas's great-grandfather was seventy years old, poor, weak and blind, he married a sixteen-year-old girl. From time to time he ran away from home. When he did he took to the road and asked to be taken anywhere. His great-granddaughter imagined him "walking through the roads dying of laughter." Like the wandering great-grandfather, when the author left Montevideo he also "took to the road, towards the unknown, clean and with no worries" (10). When he left for Buenos Aires in 1975, Galeano lost his belongings and left his people behind. In the middle of 1976 for the second time he had no alternative but to flee again. Thus the author twice left behind friends, relatives, familiar places, and jobs. He saw three important journals rise and vanish: *Marcha* and *Epoca* in Montevideo, and *Crisis* in Buenos Aires. Galeano calls attention to the fact that two million people have fled Uruguay, Chile, and Paraguay in a short period of time: "The ships sail, full of young lads who escape prison, the grave or hunger" (83). Throughout the narrative we witness the farewells, the precarious relationships, separations, and even the disintegration of a soccer team (cf. 126). The reasons for the farewells are sometimes strictly personal, or due to fate or illness; others, however, are compulsory.

Next to painful testimonies we find their counterpoint: the celebration of life. These two themes, which are already present in the book's title, give us a clue to the testimony that Galeano wants to record. In an essay the author has pointed out that "he writes because of a need for communication with others, to denounce what hurts and to share what gives happiness."[24] He mentioned for instance the singing of a girl in the subway (67), or when referring to his meeting with Salvador Allende he emphasizes that they "talked and drank a lot" (69): "*I accompanied* him to political *meetings* and *rallies,* we went *together* to soccer games; *we shared* meals and drinks, dances" (69).[25] In just two lines we find an abundance of words that express solidarity, brotherhood, and the joy of life. This theme of celebration of life can be perceived even in the most pathetic of stories. He tells us for example that Darcy Ribeiro, the Brazilian anthropologist, was dying of lung cancer, but he continued to laugh, and with his last strength "pinched the nurse's behinds" (73). Again and again he points out that encounters occur around food, drink, and conversation. "We drink beer, we eat stuffed crabs. We laugh at everything that night, at the 'Luna'" (79). The following passage illustrates his attitude:

> This barbeque with Eduardo Mignona would have had little taste if I had been alone. Somehow we make together the marvelous flavor of meat and wine. We eat and drink as if celebrating, with our mouths and at the same time with memory. At any moment one could be stopped by a bullet, or one could remain so lonely as to wish it would occur, but none of that has the least importance. (90)

Nature is looked upon in the same way: "Each grain of sand is alive, each pore of the skin is alive. A good music is born from me" (106). A visit to the market makes him rejoice with the different smells, colors, and flavors. The narrator believes in a brotherhood of men: "Among all of us, if one listens carefully, we form a single melody" (197). According to the author, the revolutionary is not in love with death but with life, in a very concrete way.

Considering these two very distinct modes, one could conclude that Galeano's book includes an aspect of what Claudio Guillén has called literature of exile in the nostalgic good memories of the past, but at the same time also reflects an aspect of the literature of counter-exile in his celebration of life and the present.

In the autobiographical episodes Galeano tells us that he has not always been this way. When he was nineteen years old he was completely disoriented, he did not believe in God. Political involvement did not alleviate his anguish and neither did writing. He tried to commit suicide, but on his way to the drugstore he was struck by a car and ended up in the hospital. Upon leaving the hospital, he saw things differently: "I saw the world for the first time and I wanted to eat it all" (48).

Accordingly, Galeano's narrative ends with a note of hope and with a note of despair. On the one hand, the rain washes away the white paint that covers the protest signs that in the old days covered the city walls, so that "little by little the stubborn words reappear" (201). On the other hand, he gives the news of another book-burning episode in Buenos Aires. If we read carefully the epigraph that prefaces the memoir, however, we can hope that decay will bring about change: "In history, as in nature, putrefaction is the laboratory of life" (Karl Marx).

Both Valdés and Galeano insist that they are telling the truth. Valdés speaks of the "documentary character of each detail" (16), and Galeano warns the reader that "everything told here happened" (5). This protestation is a recurrent theme in testimonial works, like the memoir and the diary, since the value and purpose of such works lie in the fact that for the most part the authors want to record testimonies that shed light on a historical period or individual life.[26] Nevertheless, as I have mentioned above, we must not forget that both works are literary in character. In both there is a distance between experience and narration, which implies a process of selection and organization on the part of the author-narrators, who in this case are also professional writers.

Cuerpo a cuerpo, published in 1979, is a novel, a work of fiction. The main character, Gregorio Yantorno, a journalist, is assigned to investigate a delicate and disturbing matter in exchange for a large sum of money. The investigation centers around an army officer, General Alejandro Cé. Mendiburu. The novel consists of the information that Yantorno succeeds in gathering about the activities of the general. He interviews the people closest to his subject: his children, Marcelo and Mariana, his comrades in the Army, Colonel Luis Marcelo Garmendia, Pensson, Lieutenant Rubianes (who is an illegitimate son of the general), Balestra, a lawyer, Father Moyano, Oscar Brasel, a former orderly, one of his former lovers, Elvira, and his last two lovers, Juan Carlos and Walter. The journalist also spies on the general himself: in the swimming pool, in his apartment, etc. The novel's structure is very complex. The discourse is made up of fragments that do not follow a chronological order. At the beginning it is difficult for the reader to understand what is happening, just as modern life and war are puzzling to the general.[27] There are certain sections that are transcriptions of the dialogues between the journalist and his boss, Yaco, or his colleagues, titled "I Cover My Mouth With My Hand," and others in which the past and present history of Argentina is recalled and connected with the history of the general's family. In the first part of the novel these latter sections are called "Babylon" and refer to the mass immigration that arrived in the country at the turn of the century. Among the recent immigrants are the immediate relatives of General Mendiburu. In the second part, they are called "Cutting and Dressmaking" and consist of comments by the journalist about some letters that he has received from an upper-class lady, presumably the general's wife.[28]

This novel is presented as if it were a testimonial document. The first part is called "Without Cuts," that is, without censorship, without meditation of any kind; it is simply the transcription of the documents, tape recordings and notes gathered by the journalist throughout his investigation, put together apparently without any order.

The figure of the general, with all its complexities and contradictions, weaknesses and good qualities, emerges from these interviews and other documents. We are not dealing here with a stereotype, or a simple man, but on the contrary, with a cultured man who admires Cortés, who recites Claudel, who discusses Sarmiento, who reads and rereads Marx's *The Grundrisse. Foundations of the Critique of Political Economy* as if it were his Bible. In short, we are confronted with a modern soldier who demonstrates his professionalism and military knowledge, who has traveled, attended

courses in Panama, who has been aide-de-camp during De Gaulle's visit to
Argentina; he is also a refined man, well-educated, of impeccable manners;
he speaks French. He is a man who suffered from repression under Perón in
1952 and who was jailed and confined to Patagonia, a man who does not
hesitate to kill his enemy: he killed the bodyguard who had been assigned to
spy on him and who had become dictatorial. He is also a man who can
experience fear, who feels loneliness, who talks to his parrot, who has
become impotent and has sexual relations with his subordinates, and who is
murdered while suffering from an overdose of drugs and alcohol.

While contemplating one of his medals, the one that commemorates the
battle of Ayacucho, which put an end to the wars of Independence in 1824,
General Mendiburu recalls with nostalgia those times when

> all the enemies on one side, there, in front of us, sharp and clear, lined up
> square on the hill: different uniforms, different faces, different flags. Even
> different commands. There: far away, without mingling. A different and
> distinct enemy. What an enemy that was! One needed him: one could
> even love the enemy. There. Not at my side, as now: mixed, as if stuck
> together, confusing, ripping apart each others' bellies.[29]

It is not this way now: the enemy lives in his house. In a dialogue with
Elvira, his lover, she observes: "But, we are not at war here," and the
general replies: "We are, Elvira. It is an undeclared war, Elvira" (271). This
silent war takes place even within the general's own family, as his children
do not share his convictions.[30] His daughter has become a guerrilla after
having been her father's "little soldier," and his son, who has attempted to
kill him several times, is a homosexual, which is anathema to a soldier.
When his daughter Mariana is incarcerated, the general cannot prevent it; he
is helpless. As a father he requests special conditions for his daughter, in
order that she not continue to mix with other jailed urban guerrillas. But as
a soldier he thinks that perhaps incarceration will teach her a lesson and that
it might help her forget the brainwashing to which she has been subjected
by the rebels.

In the second part of the novel, entitled "Firing Squad and Afterwards,"
the tensions between father and children, as well as the collective tensions,
are clearly outlined. In one scene Mariana confronts her father with a gun
and accuses him of being an assassin responsible for the deaths of her
comrades: Juan, Lucrecia, Rodolfo, Frida, Antonio, Paco, Marisa, Tucho,
Aldo, Graciela. She also attacks his sexual perversions, not because he is a
homosexual—her brother is also homosexual and she does not condemn
him—but because "you are one of those who gives little gifts and pays to be
had" (389).

The confusion and ambiguity that characterize modern life and war are
reflected ironically in the names of the characters. Alejandro, who is named

after a general and hero, is not heroic but impotent. Marcelo, whose name recalls Mars the god of war, is a homosexual and according to his father not a real man. And Mariana, named after the Virgin Mary, whose name is supposed to embody the essence of feminity, is a modern amazon, a guerrilla who is not afraid of challenging the military order.

Allusions to the contemporary political situation include the visit of a Dutch representative of Amnesty International to a hospital strongly guarded by soldiers in order to interview a patient who suffers the effects of the cruelest tortures. This episode is included in the narrative because Yantorno serves as an interpreter for the Dutch doctor. At the end of the novel the police search the journalist's house and destroy his books. Later Yantorno receives a menacing telephone call urging him to leave at once, as he has become dangerous; otherwise he may not be able to escape. He is punished as a miserable intellectual who writes for money. In this way the courage of the journalist and his increasing involvement in political affairs result once again in a compulsory exile.

In *Cuerpo a cuerpo* the individual, the intellectual (who is by no means a saint), confronts the might of the military, a depersonalizing institution whose motto is "subordination and order," as is repeated by the general's parrot until exhaustion.

Like *Días y noches,* Viñas's novel is also characterized by fragmented discourse. One of the unifying elements is the ubiquitous presence of the journalist, who by recording the various testimonies plays the role of memory with regard to the events of the present. Here also the information gathered by him is inserted into a larger historical framework which give his investigation a perspective.

Since the crisis of 1890, according to the army officers in the novel, the army has been the institution in charge of saving the country. Thus, in 1930, 1955, and 1966 the military each time overthrew the legitimately elected presidents and seized power. In 1972 the army returned political power to the civilians by holding elections. Héctor Cámpora was elected president and made possible Perón's return in 1973. The army intervened again in 1976 to impose order, as it had done in the past: it was one more of its campaigns to save the country. For Alejandro the present war is another frontier war, a war between civilization and barbarism. He exclaims: "Civilization and barbarism: that is our war" (418). Before it had been the Indians; now it is the urban guerrillas. But Alejandro corrects Sarmiento. He suggests that it is necessary to change the conjunction "and" for "or": "civilization or barbarism, white or black." The empty spaces left by this process of cleaning up will have to be filled by a selected immigration (419) from Rhodesia, Algeria, and Angola. This plan, however, is not perfect. One of the officers asks what will happen with the children of these people after a generation, when they become Argentinians, "Aren't they going to start kicking and screaming after a while?" (419). This dilemma is exemplified by the general's own family: his grandfather was an anarchist immigrant from Catalonia, Práxedes Clans, and the general's children, the new generation of Argentinians who are protesting against the establishment, are being phased out.

Another element that gives coherence to the discourse by giving it perspective is the use of the epigraphs. They remind the reader that the events and policies described in the novel do not constitute isolated occurrences but are part of a rationale that stems from the famous phrase by Alberdi, "to govern is to populate," and Sarmiento's "civilization and barbarism."

Alberdi's phrase acquires an ironic overtone, since the repressive "cleaning up policies" have produced a decline in the population. In one of the epigraphs we read the following statement by General Manuel Saint-Jean from 1976: "First we are going to kill all the subversives; then their collaborators; then their sympathizers; then the indifferent ones. And finally the shy ones" (367).

According to the view put forth by the novel, immigration policies have been one of the crucial factors in the historical and economical development of Argentina. Viñas's novel maintains that the policy of selective immigration has been utilized to safeguard the interests of a social class and particular ideology. This opinion is certainly not new. In a statement from 1867, in which he favored the plans of the white man and civilization, Sarmiento had already pointed this out:

> It may be very unfair to exterminate the savages, suffocate rising civilizations, conquer peoples who possess privileged lands. But thanks to this injustice, America, instead of being left to the savages, incapable of progress, is today occupied by the Caucasian race, the most beautiful and progressive of all those who people the earth. (Epigraph, *Cuerpo a cuerpo,* 41)

What is new is the view that this statement is still valid, although applied to a somewhat different reality. Saúl Sosnowski has called it the "continuation of a demythologizing project" of Argentinian official history in Viñas's novels.[31] Once more, Viñas seems to say that history repeats itself, and not by accident, since nothing is left to chance: Yantorno, the journalist, the undesirable, must leave or face the consequences for not having obeyed the rules of the white man, of civilization.

Throughout these works we find a revolutionary interpretation of history, of the social reality presented, that coincides with Foucault's description. It is suggested that by utilizing the army as an instrument the economic power of a social class has shaped history, and that it is almost impossible to defy a modern, well-trained, and intelligent army. What is under attack in that system is the freedom of thought, the freedom of expression, and above all the freedom to be different. The three narrator-protagonists are journalists, intellectuals, professionals of the word. There is no room for them in a system controlled by the military, and for this reason their only escape is exile. We are confronted here with a fight that is "body to body," but also, one could add, "mind to mind."[32]

These three works complement each other. The two testimonial narratives, the diary and the memoir, illuminate fiction by portraying a historical period. The three give testimony of the same phenomenon in different ways, since they all have as their main theme repression in the countries of the Southern Cone. The three portray the confrontation between the individual and a system of extermination. They denounce a system that annihilates the individual by reducing him to the condition of a slave, to another part of a machine that cannot work if the parts do not obey its orders.[33] Ironically, as *Cuerpo a cuerpo* emphasizes, nobody is saved, for the army as an institution also reduces the soldier to impotence. We may conclude by saying that literary testimony may sometimes be effective. As Lukács noted in an interview, his reading of the *Iliad* when he was nine years old was a decisive experience for his future development, for Hector, the man who was defeated, was right.[34]

Notes

1. See issue number 35 of *Nueva Sociedad* (March–April 1978), devoted entirely to the recent mass flow of exiles from Latin America: especially the articles by Angel Rama, "La riesgosa navegación del escritor exiliado," pp. 5–15; Noé Jitrik, "Primeros tanteos: literatura y exilio," pp. 48–55; and Renato Prada Oropeza, "(Del) exilio interno (al) exilio externo," pp. 64–67. See also, Julio Cortázar, "América Latina: exilio y literatura," *Eco* 205 (November 1978): 59–66.

2. Ana María Barrenechea, in "Las ideas de Sarmiento antes de la publicación del 'Facundo,'" *Textos hispanoamericanos, de Sarmiento a Sarduy* (Caracas: Monteávila, 1978), states that "Sarmiento fought with all his resources as a writer, had faith in the power of the word, became indignant when others did not recognize him and until the last years of his life continued to believe that his works could do more than Rosas's army" (p. 13). Furthermore, in "La configuración del 'Facundo,'" she adds that "all of Sarmiento's critics agree in emphasizing that he was not a pure creator, but rather a fighter who always used his pen to defend an idea. He himself repeated this all the time: 'Soldier, with pen or sword, I fight in order to be able to write, for to write is to think, my writing is a tool and a weapon, for fighting is to carry out thought' (in the prologue to *Campaña en el ejército grande* 14:68)," *Textos hispanoamericanos,* p. 35. The translations throughout this paper are mine.

3. (Río Piedras, Puerto Rico: Ediciones La Torre, 1963), p. 52.

4. Adalbert Dessau, in "La novela latinoamericana como conciencia histórica," *Revista Chilena de Literatura* 4 (1971): 14, establishes a difference between historical consciousness in the novel and in science.

5. (London: Harrap, 1972), p. 27.

6. *Books Abroad* 50 (Spring 1976): 272.

7. See "Nota preliminar," p. 8, in *Tejas Verdes (Diario de un campo de concentración en Chile)* 2nd ed. (Barcelona: Laia, 1978). Subsequent quotes will be indicated in the text with the number of the page in parentheses.

8. When the English translation appeared in London it was immediately and favorably reviewed in the following publications: *Times Literary Supplement,* 19 September 1975, p. 1042; *The Economist* 256, 13 September 1975, p. 124; *Spectator* 235, 13 September 1975, p. 345; *Guardian Weekly* 113, 16 November 1975, p. 26.

9. Furthermore, many readers who knew of the documentáry character of the diary referred to it as a novel. See *Tejas Verdes,* p. 10. See also Teresa Cajiao Salas, "Algunas consideraciones sobre la narrativa chilena en el exilio," *Cuadernos Hispanoamericanos* 375 (September 1981): 600–15, who emphasizes the aesthetic qualities of this work.

10. *El Tiempo* de Bogotá, "Lecturas dominicales," 24 April 1977, p. 4.

11. Ibid.

12. See ibid.

13. For a distinction between the different autobiographical genres, namely diary and memoir, see Randolph D. Pope, *La autobiografía española hasta Torres Villarroel* (Bern: Lang, 1974), pp. 3–4.

14. *Discipline and Punish. The Birth of the Prison,* trans. Alan Sheridan (New York: Pantheon, 1977), p. 304.

15. *Discipline and Punish,* p. 305. It is interesting to point out that Kenneth W. Massey, while comparing *Zoom,* an earlier novel by Valdés, and *Tejas Verdes,* concludes that in the latter "the realization of what it means for a man to be made an object becomes clear," "From behind the Bars of Signifiers and Signifieds," *Dispositio* 2, no. 1 (1977): 91.

16. Foucault, *Discipline and Punish,* p. 33.

17. Ibid., p. 47.

18. Ibid., pp. 48–49.

19. Teresa Cajiao Salas, "Algunas consideraciones sobre la narrativa chilena en el exilio," also stresses the absence of partisan considerations in Valdés's diary. She states: "Before any political difference, Valdés intends to show the tragedy of the thousands of Chileans who suffered the overwhelming burden of repression" (p. 603).

20. 12 August 1979.

21. I disagree on this point with S. R. Wilson, who considers *Días y noches* to be a novel. See "Eduardo Galeano: Exile and a Silenced Montevideo," *Chasqui* 9, no. 2–3 (February–May 1980): 33. In his review of *Días y noches,* however, Wilson asserts that "more than a novel, *Días y noches* is a chronicle that moves from Buenos Aires to Montevideo" (*Journal of Spanish Studies: Twentieth Century* 8, no. 1–2 [1980]: 192).

22. *Días y noches de amor y de guerra,* 4th ed. (Barcelona: Laia, 1979), p. 127. Hereafter citations will be indicated in the text.

23. "Defensa de la palabra," *El Tiempo* de Bogotá, "Lecturas dominicales," 24 April 1977, p. 4.

24. Ibid., p. 2.

25. Italics are mine.

26. Like Valdés, Galeano also expresses a desire to move the reader with his writings, in order that they be effective. In an interview with Hortensia Campanella, *Nueva Estafeta* 15 (February 1980): 53, he declares: "The proof that a book is useful is that the result has to do with the intention. And it is also of importance that it is worth reading: the proof of a book's effectiveness resides in its reader. A book may be read by a person and then he continues to be the same as he was. He has not changed a bit, and the book has not triggered his imagination, intelligence, creative capabilities; it has not turned on his conscience nor the capacity to doubt or reflect or dream. Then that book is useless." For Galeano, literature is a form of action; see ibid., p. 56.

27. In his review of the novel, Joao Gonçalves points out that "the novel is not easy to read; the first chapters—and one could even say the first two parts—are hard to read. At times some of the well-known names (De Gaulle, Yrigoyen, Perón . . .) provide a frame of reference that awakens interest in the reading; in others the disconnection is almost absolute" (*Chasqui* 9, no. 2–3 [February–May 1980]: 92). However, I would like to remind any prospective readers of what another reviewer said of the novel: "*Cuerpo a cuerpo* is, without a doubt, the best literary and intellectual product to come out of the Argentinian exile since 1976" (Antonio Marimón, Mexico 1979, quoted on the book jacket). Just as the journalist elucidates the story of the general in the novel, the reader must unravel this information from the text. Juan Carlos Tealdi

suggests that the complicated literary structure of this novel may have to do with the author's need as a creative writer to detach himself from the atrocities that were being committed by the military at the time he was writing his novel. Tealdi adds that although *Cuerpo a cuerpo* requires careful attention on the part of the reader, the text successfully accomplishes Viñas's project (*Borges y Viñas [Literatura e ideología]* [Madrid: Orígenes, 1983], p. 133).

28. As he has done in previous novels, in *Cuerpo a cuerpo* Viñas refers to the modern history of Argentina. He declared in an interview: "I would say that the most immediate thematic element of that series of novels is to narrate what I consider key moments of Argentina's modern period, from the Argentina that emerges as a result of the great bourgeois-liberal project" (Mario Szichman, "Entrevista a David Viñas," *Hispamérica* 1, no. 1 [1972]: 61.

29. *Cuerpo a cuerpo* (Mexico City: Siglo XXI, 1979), p. 274. Hereafter citations will be indicated in the text.

30. It is interesting to note here that in his play *Maniobras* (Buenos Aires: Ediciones Cepe, 1974), Viñas developed a very similar plot. An army general is confronted by his son and daughter, who accuse him of being responsible for the deaths of their comrades. The play ends when the guerrillas come to get him at his house.

31. See *"Jauría,* de David Viñas: continuación de un proyecto desmitificador," *Revista de Crítica Literaria Latinoamericana* 7–8 (1978): 165–72.

32. Juan Carlos Tealdi writes that *Cuerpo a cuerpo* shows that "the writer's task is rendered useless before such an overwhelming reality and the only thing he can do is to write about things that cannot be done, to write for money or to keep quiet." It is the total annihilation of the writer's purposes. *Borges y Viñas,* p. 160.

33. I agree with Ellen McCracken's reading of the novel when she states in her review of *Cuerpo a cuerpo* that "the novel develops the theme of the writer as a militant," but I do not share her view that due to the abundance of detail and lack of selectivity "the novel loses much of the critical strength that Viñas tries to emphasize" (*Hispamérica* 27 [1980]: 121–22). On the contrary, the characterization of "El Payo," the general, as a vulnerable human being corresponds to that "demythologizing project" Saúl Sosnowski described when analyzing *Jauría.*

34. From a conversation with Hans Heinz Hok, quoted by Fritz J. Raddatz, *Georg Lukács,* trans. José Francisco Ivars (Madrid: Alianza, 1975), p. 99.

Contributors

ROBERT EDWARDS completed his doctorate in comparative literature at the University of California at Riverside in 1972 as a Woodrow Wilson Dissertation Fellow. Currently he is Professor and Chairman of the English department at the State University of New York at Buffalo and a member of the Comparative Literature Program. In addition to numerous articles on medieval literature he has published *The Montecassino Passion and the Poetics of Medieval Drama* (1977) and *The Poetry of Guido Guinizelli* (1986), a translation and critical edition. He has finished a study of medieval lyric and narrative poetry, *Voices and Kinds,* and is working on a book on Chaucer.

MARÍA-INÉS LAGOS-POPE received her Ph.D. from Columbia University in 1980. She is Assistant Professor of Spanish and Latin American Studies at the University Center at Binghamton, State University of New York. She has published articles in *Revista Iberoamericana, Symposium, Hispamérica, Bilingual Review,* and in other publications. She is currently working on a book about Latin American women writers.

GIUSEPPE MAZZOTTA is Professor of Italian at Yale University. He has taught at Cornell, the University of Toronto, and the Graduate Center of the City University of New York. He is the author of *Dante, Poet of the Desert* (Princeton University Press, 1979), *The World at Play: A Study of Boccaccio's Decameron* (Princeton, 1986), and *Dante and the Acts of Discourse* (Princeton, in press).

ROSMARIE T. MOREWEDGE is Assistant Professor of German at the University Center at Binghamton, State University of New York. She is the editor of *The Role of Woman in the Middle Ages* (SUNY Press, 1975).

GEORGE O'BRIEN was born in Ireland and educated at Ruskin College, Oxford, and at the University of Warwick, England. He has held teaching positions at Warwick, Clare College, Cambridge, and at Vassar College. At present he is Assistant Professor of English at Georgetown University. He has published fiction and criticism in this country, England, and Ireland, and

138

has recently published a memoir, *The Village of Longing. An Irish Boyhood in the Fifties.*

RANDOLPH D. POPE is Professor of Spanish at Washington University in St. Louis. He has taught at Vassar College, Dartmouth, the University of Bonn in West Germany, and Barnard College. He is the author of *La autobiografía española hasta Torres Villarroel* (Bern: Lang, 1974), *Novela de emergencia: España 1939–1954* (Madrid: SGEL, 1984), and of numerous articles on Latin American and Spanish literature. He is one of the three founding and principal editors of Ediciones del Norte and has been editor of *Revista de Estudios Hispánicos* and Director of the Spanish Summer School at Middlebury College (1983–1986).

SANDRO STICCA received his Ph.D. from Columbia University in 1966. He is professor of French and Comparative Literature at the University Center at Binghamton, State University of New York. His field of expertise is the theater of the Middle Ages in a European context. He is the author of *The Latin Passion Play. Its Origins and Development* (1970), *The Medieval Drama* (1972), *The Christos Paschon and the Bizantin Theatre* (1974), *Pietro Celestino e la tradizione eremitica* (1982), *Il Planctus Mariae nella tradizione drammatica del Medio Evo* (1984), and numerous essays on French, English, Italian, Spanish and German literature.